CONCISE GUIDE TO

# Treatment of Alcoholism and Addictions

Richard J. Frances, M.D.

Vice Chairman and
Professor of Clinical Psychiatry
Department of Psychiatry
University of Medicine and Dentistry of New Jersey
New Jersey Medical School
Newark, New Jersey

John E. Franklin, Jr., M.D.

Assistant Professor of Psychiatry
Department of Psychiatry
University of Medicine and Dentistry of New Jersey
New Jersey Medical School
Newark, New Jersey

American
Psychiatric
Press, Inc.

1400 K Street, N.W.
Washington, DC 20005

Copyright © 1989 American Psychiatric Press, Inc.
ALL RIGHTS RESERVED
Manufactured in the United States of America

89  90  91  92  5  4  3  2  1

The paper used in this publication meets the minimum require-
ments of the American National Standard for Information Sciences—Permanence of Paper for Printed Library Materials,
ANSI Z39.48-1984.                                        ∞

**Library of Congress Cataloging-in-Publication Data**
Frances, Richard J.
    Concise guide to treatment of alcoholism and addictions /
    Richard J. Frances, John E. Franklin, Jr.
        p.    cm.—(Concise guides / American Psychiatric
    Press)
    Includes bibliographies and index.
    ISBN 0-88048-326-1 (alk. paper)
    1. Substance abuse—Treatment. 2. Alcoholism—
Treatment. I. Franklin, John E., 1954–      . II. Title.
III. Series: Concise guides (American Psychiatric Press)
    [DNLM: 1. Alcoholism—therapy. 2. Substance
Dependence—therapy. WM 274 F815c]
RC564.F73   1989
616.86′06—dc19
DNLM/DLC
for Library of Congress                              89-413
                                                      CIP

To the founding members of the American Academy of Psychiatrists in Alcoholism and Addictions, who have had the courage to make a difference, and to our families who have had to accept our workaholism.

# CONTENTS

# INTRODUCTION

*to the American Psychiatric Press Concise Guides*

The *American Psychiatric Press Concise Guides* series provides, in a most accessible format, practical information for psychiatrists—and especially for psychiatry residents and medical students—working in such varied treatment settings as inpatient psychiatry services, outpatient clinics, consultation/liaison services, and private practice. The *Concise Guides* are meant to complement the more detailed information to be found in lengthier psychiatry texts.

The *Concise Guides* address topics of greatest concern to psychiatrists in clinical practice. The books in this series contain a detailed Table of Contents, along with an index, tables, and charts, for easy access; and their size, designed to fit into a lab coat pocket, makes them a convenient source of information. The number of references has been limited to those most relevant to the material presented.

The treatment of patients with alcohol and drug abuse disorders is an important clinical problem for psychiatrists. As Drs. Frances and Franklin indicate in their preface, alcohol and drug treatment admissions amount to approximately 1.6 million per year at a cost exceeding $1.6 billion. With an estimated 14 million alcoholics in the United States, and with increasing abuse among younger people of psychoactive substances such as "crack" and cocaine, a knowledge of appropriate management with alcohol and drug disorders is essential.

The authors of this *Concise Guide* are nationally prominent clinicians and educators in the field of alcoholism and the addictions. Dr. Frances was the founder and first president of the American Academy of Psychiatrists in Alcoholism and Addictions (AAPAA). Dr. Frances has lectured widely and written extensively about the difficulties of managing and treating patients with these disorders. During his 10-year period in overseeing the alcohol and drug treatment program at the New York Hospital, Cornell University Westchester Division, Dr. Frances has not only treated thousands of patients with substance abuse disorders, but has supervised hundreds of psychiatry residents and other mental health care workers in the proper treatment of patients with these disorders. Dr. Franklin has worked closely with Dr. Frances in designing outpatient treatment and rehabilitation programs for these patients. They have teamed up to write outstanding chapters for major textbooks. In particular, they wrote the chapter on Alcohol-Induced Organic Mental Disorders for the nationally acclaimed *The American Psychiatric Press Textbook of Neuropsychiatry*, and they teamed up again to write the chapter on Alcohol and Other Psychoactive Substance Use Disorders for *The American Psychiatric Press Textbook of Psychiatry*. They have demonstrated a remarkable ability to integrate complex and diffuse material in a coherent, understandable fashion.

As implied in the title of the book, emphasis is on treatment. However, Drs. Frances and Franklin begin their *Concise Guide* by discussing the magnitude of the problem, with emphasis on the economic costs, medical and psychiatric complications, and problems with denial. They also summarize major developmental issues occurring in the field, including the evolution of the disease concept of alcoholism and a much greater, recent emphasis on prevention.

The authors next turn to important issues concerning the diagnosis of selected alcohol or substance use disorders. They begin this section by discussing some of the trends that led to the development of the DSM-III-R classification system and summarize work that is in progress in the development of the ICD-10 and DSM-IV nomenclature for substance use disorders. As they emphasize, the evolution of the new classification systems has resulted in part from major advances in understanding the biologic causes and psychosocial sequelae of drug and alcohol abuse and dependency. They then discuss the criteria used to diagnose substance dependence and abuse and also outline in detail many of the organic mental disorders associated with alcoholism and the addictions.

The authors next consider substance abuse disorders in two specific environments: the general hospital and the workplace. Various laboratory tests and diagnostic instruments are also presented.

Drs. Frances and Franklin summarize the various clinical features associated with alcohol, opioids, cocaine, amphetamines, phencyclidine, cannabis, nicotine, and inhalants. They then proceed to discuss treatment approaches to alcoholism and other psychoactive substance use disorders. Their emphasis in this section is on differential therapeutics, the role of abstinence, selection of setting, treatment of intoxication and overdose, withdrawal and detoxification, polysubstance abuse, and rehabilitation. They also discuss various treatment options: individual therapy, group therapy, psychopharmacology, family therapy, self-help groups, activity therapy, counseling, and education. Also considered are dual-diagnosis patients, outcome studies, and relapse.

The last section is devoted to treatment of special populations: women; children and adolescents; the elderly; chronic, handicapped, and homeless patients; and minorities. This section is especially helpful because the focus of most chapters is on the relatively healthy adult patient.

The authors have included 24 tables that highlight important information to which the reader will readily turn when treatment questions arise. Purchasers of this book should be pleased with the clear and precise prose and the practical and clinically relevant orientation of this book.

I have been fortunate to have edited chapters prepared by Drs. Frances and Franklin in the past. I can state unequivocally that the material contained in this book is new and is of the highest quality. They have included a number of 1988 references and have made a thorough and careful review of the literature. They readily acknowledge controversies in the field and provide rational explanation for the treatment recommendations that they select.

Drs. Richard Frances and John Franklin have prepared an outstanding *Concise Guide to Treatment of Alcoholism and Addictions*. This beautifully written, pocket-size book should be of invaluable assistance to psychiatrists and other mental health professionals involved in the management of alcohol and substance use disorders. Readers should find this guide an excellent addition to their practical, medical library. I recommend it highly for psychiatry residents and medical students who need access to information quickly and efficiently.

Robert E. Hales, M.D.
Series Editor
*American Psychiatric Press Concise Guides*

# PREFACE

In the United States, it is estimated that there are 14 million alcoholics. Alcohol and drug client treatment admissions amount to approximately 1.6 million per year, with total costs for alcohol and drug treatment totaling more than 1.6 billion dollars. Alcoholism accounts for three-fourths of the admissions and three-fourths of these are for outpatient treatment. Those in every category of health care—physicians, nurses, psychologists, social workers, alcohol and drug counselors, and activity therapists—and students in all of these areas are constantly faced with treatment choices and options that are critical to the care of patients with psychoactive substance disorders.

This handbook is designed to be a concise guide containing useful tools for the choices and options of treatment employed by these professionals. Although primarily written with the professional in mind, many allied helping professions such as the clergy, educators, lawyers, and police officers will find this volume useful. Medical education about the addictions has been increasing in recent years for health professionals. However, considering the magnitude of the problem, this area remains underrepresented in the core of medical student and resident curriculums.

This concise overview of treatment issues is relevant to the clinician in the trenches and is a distillation of our clinical experience as well as our review of the literature. During a 10-year period at New York Hospital, Cornell University Westchester Division, Richard Frances, M.D., had the opportunity to follow the treatment course and progress of 2,500 inpatients with substance disorders and to supervise approximately 200 psychiatric residents, both individually and in their teams. At both Cornell and the New Jersey Medical School, John Franklin, M.D., has worked extensively with outpatient treatment planning for this population. The limitations of a handbook format, in terms of summarizing and highlighting the important issues, lead us to focus on what we feel is the most important clinically relevant material, at the risk of omitting extensive presentations of research data and reviews of literature. We are grateful to Robert Hales, M.D., Carol Nadelson, M.D., and Ron McMillen for their suggestions regarding the book; to our colleagues, staff, and students, both at Cornell Westchester Division and the New Jersey Medical School; and to our patients who have worked with us at understanding treatment problems. We also want to thank Roberta Shepherd for her patience and assistance in preparing the manuscript and for her editorial comments. Our department Chairman, Sheldon Miller, M.D., provided wise counsel and much support. Finally, without encouragement from Marsha and Arline, the work would not have been possible.

Richard J. Frances, M.D.
John E. Franklin, Jr., M.D.

# INTRODUCTION 1

Paralleling a vast increase in public interest in substance disorder treatment, researchers and health professionals have made a wide variety of modalities, settings, and approaches to treatment available in this population of patients in the past decade. There has been an explosion of knowledge regarding the biopsychosocial aspects of substance disorders. Patients, their families, and clinicians still often face confusing choices about the best combination of treatments tailored to their individual needs. Final answers about optimal choice of treatment will await valid and well-constructed outcome research; the current literature on substance disorder treatment outcome is relatively sparse, nonspecific, and of only limited usefulness to the clinician. The clinician's choices are enhanced by a careful history, by mental status and physical examinations, by diagnostic formulation, and by confirmatory evidence from laboratory tests and third-party sources (e.g., family members, employers, teachers, probation officers, and other professionals).

## ■ CONFRONTING DENIAL

Helping the patient to recognize a problem and to accept help are the two most important steps in treatment recognized both by self-help groups and by professionals. This is frequently difficult because of the nature of addictive disorders, which leads to denial, lying, and organicity. Both the patient and the therapist may be struggling with the stigma of substance disorders and with accepting that the patient has an illness. Most patients will have a wish to achieve controlled use and will have difficulty accepting the therapist's standard of abstinence as the goal for treatment. Patients frequently feel hopeless about ever achieving sustained abstinence and need to be encouraged that the goal is attainable. Seeing others who are recovering and personal experience of increasing periods of abstinence help improve hope. Drug substitution (e.g., methadone maintenance) and the use of other medications when indicated may be met with resistance that will often need to be worked through (1).

## ■ FORMING AN ALLIANCE

Having frequently grown up in families with substance disorders, it is not surprising that the patient with a substance problem is likely to have typical transference resistances to treatment and to evoke countertransference reactions in the therapist that may either facilitate or negate treatment, depending on how these reactions are handled. Therapists who are well-informed and well-trained and who understand and are in touch with their own feelings are more helpful to patients and less likely to experience "burnout" (2).

## ■ ATTRIBUTES AND ATTITUDES OF THE THERAPIST

Ten attributes and attitudes are helpful in working with patients with substance disorders (Table 1):

1. The most crucial nonspecific variable is a caring relationship. Often underestimated in importance, a concern for patients and a willingness to form an active therapeutic alliance (with some degree of therapeutic zeal, yet without overidentification) are crucial to work with patients who have substance disorders. An empathic capacity to feel the patient's experience and yet to maintain objectivity is crucial. A tradition in psychotherapy that goes back to Ferenczi and Alexander of

TABLE 1. **Attributes of Therapists that Facilitate Substance Disorder Treatment**

- Caring relationship
- Informed optimism
- Capacity to tolerate anxiety, depression
- Flexibility
- Knowledge of addictions
- Intellectual curiosity
- Wisdom
- Persistence and patience
- Capacity to listen
- Honesty and integrity

activity and of creating an environment in which a patient can achieve comfort and growth is desirable. This includes an ability to confront with concern as well as to provide emotional support in appropriate ways. This does not mean playing a real sexual or parental role or taking on a contrived position that is not genuinely felt by the therapist.

2. The therapist should be an informed optimist. It has been said that the difference between an optimist and a pessimist is that the pessimist is better informed. However, therapeutic nihilism or overidentification with a patient's helplessness, low self-esteem, and hopelessness often contributes to poor treatment results. An informed optimism based on the experience of having helped patients, on knowledge of the course and treatment of addictions, and on the experience of working with patients who have done well is a tremendous asset to any therapist. Acceptance of the limits of treatment and of the chronicity that is frequently part of the illness, however, is equally important.

3. The therapist's capacity to tolerate anxiety, pain, frustration, and depression is essential and may aid in the patients identifying with these qualities without using substances. When therapists are unaware of their own weaknesses and sensitive areas, they may find themselves colluding with the patients in avoiding painful areas. Therapists who know themselves and can tolerate depression are also able to work with more difficult cases.

4. Flexibility and open-mindedness are desirable therapist traits. Simple answers to complicated problems applied uniformly without taking into account special circumstances are often wrong. Dogmatically held positions by therapists and treatment programs often may lead to blind spots, facilitate splitting, and recreate an atmosphere of conflict already familiar in patients' lives. Flexibility can involve bringing together several modalities of treatment, sequentially using clinical trials of different modalities, and willingness to seek out consultation and supervision in difficult cases. The setting of strict limits and providing a consistency of approach can occur along with the kind of flexibility discussed here.

5. In addition to good general knowledge of psychiatry, a good knowledge of the addictions and their treatment modalities is

essential. Resourcefulness, creativity, and knowledge about a number of modalities of treatment with a good theoretical grounding in at least several is extremely helpful.

6. Intellectual curiosity is vital to the therapist's growth. It is essential that the therapist keep up with the clinical and research literature. The therapist should have an active interest and curiosity in learning more about the needs of each patient.

7. Wisdom is found in the best therapists. This may grow with the therapist's work and life experience and is enhanced by humility and a sense of humor. Many fine therapists use metaphors in ways that capture an image of immense usefulness to the patient. The eminent behavioral psychologist, Howard Hunt, once told an acting-out polysubstance abuser that he was behaving like a loose cannon on the deck of a rolling wooden ship in a storm. He compared a self-defeating alcoholic patient to a child who was always reaching for ice cream cones only to have them melt before they reached his lips. Perhaps wisdom is best described in the serenity prayer, which seeks "serenity to accept the things I cannot change, courage to change the things I can, and wisdom to know the difference."

8. Persistence and patience are qualities that are as valuable to clinicians as they are to researchers. Like a fisherman chasing a marlin, the therapist must be able to wait, to work hard, and to be prepared for either little or late ultimate gratification from the case.

9. The capacity to listen and to watch both what is and is not said and to act accordingly is very important. This includes sharing with the patient what has been heard. "You listen but you don't hear," "you don't listen," "you aren't seeing what I am really like," may or may not be told to the therapist. The statements may be true or they may represent the way the patient felt about parents or other figures in the patient's life. Because of denial, signs and symptoms of problems need to be closely watched. In the substance disorder field, perhaps because of the emphasis on psychoeducation and counseling, the basic skills of listening always need to be emphasized.

10. Honesty and integrity in the therapist and in the treatment team are crucial. Extremely sensitive to deception and fre-

quently mistrustful, the patient will need to have an ongoing consistent experience with a therapist worthy of trust. In working with patients with substance disorders who have had a regression or erosion of their value systems, examination of values almost inevitably becomes part of treatment. The therapist's integrity becomes an important asset in this exploration. Common and sometimes subtle forms of corruption of the treatment can occur and must be carefully avoided. The team approach frequently can lead to an open and honest discussion, which may help individuals face their own countertransference issues and may strengthen the total treatment approach.

## ■ POTENTIAL ABUSES IN THE TREATMENT OF SUBSTANCE DISORDERS

The following are examples of more or less subtle forms of corruption that individual therapists and treatment programs must attempt to avoid and to manage if they occur.

1. Preferential treatment influenced by VIP pressures, resulting in mistakes and splitting in the team.
2. Distortions of diagnosis (e.g., underdiagnosis of alcoholism because of fears or pressure).
3. Admission of patients or extending length of stay to fill beds without clear indications.
4. Ordering of excessive laboratory tests or diagnostic measures and overcharging for services.
5. Excessively punitive or critical approaches, with constant threats of discharge in patients who are resistant to treatment.
6. Breaches of confidentiality, leading to major problems in trust.

## ■ REFERENCES

1. Newman RG: Methadone treatment: defining and evaluating success. N Engl J Med 1987; 317:447–450
2. Frances RJ, Alexopoulos GS: Patient management and education; getting the alcoholic into treatment. Physician and Patient 1982; 1(6):9–14

# 2 MAGNITUDE OF THE PROBLEM

## ■ EPIDEMIOLOGY

Standardized interviews were used in a five-city epidemiologic catchment area (ECA) study to determine the incidence and prevalence of psychiatric disorders (1). Psychoactive substance use disorders placed first among 15 DSM-III (2) diagnoses, with an average of 13.6 percent of the general population sampled having a lifetime prevalence of alcohol abuse and dependence and approximately 5.9 percent having other drug abuse. Six-month prevalence rates were found to be approximately 5 percent for alcohol abuse or dependence and 1 to 2 percent for other drug abuse. Higher prevalence was found in more rural regions among those with poorer education. The incidence of abuse of alcohol among males is two- to fourfold higher than among females in the United States. This ratio (e.g., 28 to 1 for Koreans) varies significantly across cultures. Alcoholism tends to begin between the ages of 16 and 30; the onset of alcoholism in individuals older than 50 is lower. There has been a somewhat declining prevalence of alcohol use in high school seniors to 65 percent in 1985 and a declining daily use to 4.8 percent; 37 percent of high school seniors have had five or more drinks in a row at least once in the last two weeks (3).

Alcohol and drug use, abuse, and dependence have a vast impact on our culture and society. In addition to being the nation's number one public health problem, the public is increasingly aware of addiction's major effects on the economic, political, and social fabric of American cultural life. Measures of the dimension of the problem include per capita consumption, lifetime prevalence, the number of current cases, morbidity and mortality, fetal alcohol syndrome, fetal effects of other drugs, health care costs, and total cost of lost work time. Surveys of incidence among the mentally ill have found that 30 to 55 percent have chemical abuse problems (4). If hysteria was the most talked about psychiatric problem of the late 19th century, the mentally ill chemically abusing patient is the leading challenge for psychiatry in the 1990s.

## ALCOHOL

High levels of divorce and separation are associated both with alcoholism and with being the child of an alcoholic. Rates of alcoholism vary among cultures; they are higher in the Soviet Union, France, Scandinavia, Ireland, and Korea and lower in China and in Islamic and Mediterranean cultures. The average American over age 14 annually consumes 2.77 gallons of absolute alcohol: the equivalent of approximately 2.2 oz of vodka a day. Despite an overall decline in total alcohol consumption, problems related to alcohol remain the most common and costly. Approximately one-tenth of those who drink consume half the alcohol sold. It has been estimated that 100,000 deaths per year are alcohol related, with liver disease ranking as the fourth leading cause of death. Alcoholism is the leading associated factor for cirrhosis, which accounts for 31,500 deaths annually in the United States, even though less than 10 percent of alcoholics develop cirrhosis. The suicide rate for alcoholism is approximately 15 percent and is 15-fold that of suicide in the general population. There is a high association between alcohol and/or drug use, abuse, and addiction and violent crime (including assault, rape, child molestation, and attempted murder). Approximately 25,000 die and 150,000 are permanently disabled in alcohol-related traffic accidents (5). Approximately 25 percent of patients admitted to general hospitals have alcohol-related problems. In addition, alcohol- and drug-related morbidity (including effects of intoxication, overdose, withdrawal, chronic use, and medical complications) is often underdiagnosed in the general hospital. Withdrawal symptoms are especially dangerous, accompanied by medical problems such as pneumonia, liver failure, and subdural hematomas.

## COCAINE

The past decade has seen approximately a fivefold increase to 25–40 million Americans who have tried cocaine. Increased marketing pressures, lower prices, and availability of more potent, fast-acting cocaine derivatives that can be smoked or used intravenously (iv) (e.g., "crack") have increased experimentation, availability, and prevalence of dependence. In the 1970s, experimentation with cocaine was considered relatively safe by many young people and was thought to be not very dangerous even by some addictions experts. Cocaine psychosis was rarely reported; lower dosages of cocaine were used and rarely led to reports of major complications. In the 1980s, increased market demand for cocaine was accompanied by increased availability in purer, more potent forms at lower prices and with more rapid routes of administration, contributing to more frequent severe complications, telescoping of the course, and wider problems across social class and race. In the past decade, emergency room visits and medical-examiner-reported deaths associated with cocaine use have increased fourfold. Males and females have an approximate equal incidence of cocaine addiction; there has been an increasing prevalence among all socioeconomic groups. In 1985, 17 percent of high school seniors had experimented with cocaine as compared to 5.6 percent in 1975, an almost threefold increase (6). Thirty percent of 27-year-olds have tried cocaine. In adolescents, cocaine addiction is telescoped with progression from use to addiction being reduced from four years in adults to one and a half years in adolescents (7).

## AN INTERNATIONAL PROBLEM

Cocaine consumption has leaped from an estimated 35 to 41 million metric tons in 1981 to 50 to 61 million metric tons in 1984. In the late 1980s, drug addiction has become the leading concern of the American public. The influence of drug abuse in terms of crime and other forms of corruption has contributed to drug abuse becoming a major election issue. Spread of acquired immune deficiency syndrome (AIDS) through iv drug use poses a major threat to the nation's health. The international drug trade has led to enormous problems for Latin American and Asian countries in which farmers depend heavily on the economic value of drug-related crops, governments are corrupted by the consequences of this economic dependence, and indigenous populations are faced with high availability of coca leaves and coca paste. Border control and law enforcement efforts have not been successful at reducing availability. Inadequate resources have been devoted to prevention and treatment to reduce demand. Media have taken a lead in raising public consciousness about myths related to cocaine and in increasing awareness that cocaine is a highly addictive and destructive drug.

## AMPHETAMINES

Amphetamines are compounds with stimulant-reinforcing effects similar to those of cocaine. Diversion and abuse of amphetamines, which were prescribed often in the treatment of narcolepsy, weight disorders, and depressive disorders, peaked in the 1960s. With more careful control of amphetamines, legal use, diversion, and illegal use have declined.

## AIDS AND IV DRUGS

The iv use of opioids and cocaine has been a major risk factor in the spread of AIDS through needle sharing and disinhibition of risk-taking behavior. This can take the form of sexual behavior with multiple partners who are not well known to the individual and not following recommendations for safe sex (e.g., use of condoms). Female addicts and sexual partners of addicts, who are human immunodeficiency virus (HIV) positive have the added risk of AIDS spreading to fetuses. In Newark, New Jersey, one in 25 children are born to HIV positive mothers, mostly as a result of spread of AIDS through iv addiction. Approximately 50 percent of iv addicts in the New York area and as many as 65 percent in Newark were HIV positive in 1988; rates in Philadelphia were 14 percent and in Los Angeles 4 percent. Sites vary greatly where they fit on a spectrum of rates of infectivity and numbers of addicts at specific stages of the illness, with the urban poor and minorities being hardest hit by iv needle sharing. Continued iv use of cocaine in addicts maintained on methadone makes it harder to reduce HIV spread even in relatively compliant methadone maintenance populations.

## OPIOIDS

In 1980 there were approximately 492,000 opioid addicts in the United States, a number that has remained stable (8). It is difficult to obtain accurate data on drug use in any population; estimates come from overdose reports, surveys, prevalence of medical complications, arrests, and admissions into treatment programs. Current heroin abuse is more frequently a problem in urban males and in the 18- to 25-year-old group. A higher incidence of nonmedical use of opioids other than heroin is found among whites (12 versus 7 percent for minorities). Minorities have twice the number of heroin abusers as the general population. This statistic may be skewed because of admissions to public treatment facilities and because there may be substantial numbers of white middle-class addicts who are less likely to be detected by the means of surveying incidence. Greater psychopathology is found in cultural groups in which heroin is less endemic.

In addition to lacking adequate availability of treatment openings, most methadone programs suffer from lack of capacity for intensive treatment, including enough individual and group counseling, a team approach, and the increasingly important medical and psychiatric support needed to deal with this massive problem. Unfortunately, most patients with psychoactive substance use disorders, including narcotics addicts, are not in treatment.

## *TOBACCO*

A 1988 surgeon general's report highlights the massive effects of tobacco addiction, which continues to be one of the leading preventable health problems in the United States and accounts for 300,000 deaths per year (9). Approximately 25 percent of Americans smoke tobacco, at an annual expense of $23 billion. Dependence on tax revenues, which amounted to $8 billion in 1980, leads to resistance to tighter regulations in tobacco use. Although cigarette use is decreasing in men to approximately 35 percent, it has grown in women to 30 percent. Educational campaigns, self-help groups, self-help literature, treatment facilities, and government legislation have been aimed at decreasing the numbers of smokers. Smoking in public places (e.g., restaurants, airplanes, hospitals, and work environments) is becoming increasingly restricted, and the rights of nonsmokers are being considered.

## PHENCYCLIDINE

Phencyclidine (PCP) or "angel dust" began to be used as a street drug in the 1960s and had become more commonly abused in the 1970s. In certain eastern areas, PCP abuse is epidemic and is frequently associated with violent and bizarre behavior.

## HALLUCINOGENS

Lysergic acid diethylamide (LSD) achieved its greatest popularity in the 1960s and 1970s and has begun once again to become popular in some high school communities among students. Some students have discovered that LSD is not easily detectable in urine samples. LSD use has increased in some subcultures. In the 1960s psychedelic drugs were romanticized as part of a cultural movement that included a style of mind expansion and a poetical expression in rock culture, and became associated with turning away from war, rebelling against society, and "dropping out." Southwest American Indians had long used psilocybin 21 in religious ceremonies. LSD has been the most popular of the psychedelic drugs; however, new synthetic derivatives such as 3,4-methylenedioxyamphetamine (MDA) and 3,4-methylenedioxymethamphetamine are also abused. Psychedelics seem to be decreasing in popularity. In 1979, 7.1 percent of 12- to 17-year-olds and 25 percent of 18- to 25-year-olds tried it. By 1982, rates had dropped to 5 and 21 percent, respectively (10).

## MARIJUANA

Cannabis has been widely used throughout the world as a recreational drug. Increased potency and heavy use have led to increasingly medical and psychological risk. In 1979, more than 50 million people had used marijuana at least once. Marijuana is a frequently abused substance among adolescents, with 21 percent of young teenagers and 40 percent of young adults having tried marijuana in 1982. Marijuana use peaked among adolescents in the 1970s; daily marijuana use by adolescents had fallen to 5 percent in 1982. Regular use of marijuana has increasingly been disapproved of in surveys of adolescents. Marijuana continues to be a gateway drug for other substances of abuse.

## INHALANTS

In 1980, 10 percent of 12- to 17-year-olds had abused inhalants at least once. Among the abusable inhalants are gasoline, airplane glue, nitrous oxide, amyl nitrite, butyl nitrite, and a variety of cleaning fluids. These substances tend to be used more by socioeconomically deprived young males 13 to 15 years old and in certain subcultures (e.g., American and Mexican Indians). A subset of the homosexual community has been abusing amyl nitrite since the 1970s. Inhalant intoxication has been closely associated with aggressive, disruptive, antisocial behavior and is associated with a poor performance in school, increased family disruption, and other drug abuse.

## DEPRESSANTS

Although there has been a decline in abuse of benzodiazepines and sedative hypnotics, these useful medications frequently have a potential for abuse and dependence. Approximately 15 percent of the US population used a benzodiazepine in 1986, with a ratio of female to male use and white to black use at approximately 3 to 1. Approximately one to six users abuse sedatives, which may be iatrogenically induced or through diverted supplies. Barbiturate overdoses, once frequently the cause of emergency room visits, have decreased because of decreasing popularity of barbiturate prescription and use. Benzodiazepines have been more frequently prescribed than barbiturates, partly because of their higher index of therapeutic safety and lesser chance of causing respiratory depression. However, interaction between benzodiazepine use and use of opioids can potentiate central nervous system (CNS) depression.

Physicians prescribing benzodiazepines need to be aware of potential for abuse, especially in individuals with risk factors of alcohol and drug problems. It is difficult to get a clear incidence and prevalence of alcoholism and other drug abuse because of a lack of clear criteria for diagnosis of dependence, variations of subpopulations studies, tolerance of a particular subculture for drug-related behaviors, and dishonesty of reporting of substance problems.

## *POLYSUBSTANCE PROBLEMS*

Recently, polysubstance abuse has increased, with combined use of alcohol, heroin, cocaine, methadone, and tobacco. Combinations of use of substances have been especially noted in young patients and females. Teenagers tend to progress from alcohol and tobacco use to marijuana use and use of barbiturates, codeine, or other opioids before abusing heroin. Deaths related to overdose are more commonly associated with combinations of alcohol, depressants, and heroin than with cocaine, which has recently received greater public attention.

## ■ ECONOMIC COST

In 1986, expenditures for alcohol and drug treatment and prevention services totaled $1.6 billion; estimates of total medical cost for alcoholism range as high as $15 billion (State Alcohol and Drug Abuse Profile, unpublished data, 1988 fiscal year). It is impossible to calculate the hidden cost related to corruption, crime, and lost work potential due to drug and alcohol abuse. In 1983, it was estimated that alcohol abuse cost the United States almost $117 billion; this includes $71 billion attributed to lost employment and reduced productivity and $15 billion due to health care cost (11). Other related costs include motor vehicle crashes, crime, social welfare costs, and indirect costs such as victims of crime, costs of incarceration due to alcohol- and drug-related crimes, and motor vehicle crashes in terms of time as well as property lost. The costs for drug abuse are approximately one-half of those for alcoholism, with higher cost related to crime and lower cost estimates for reduced productivity and employment, probably related to the smaller numbers of drug abusers compared to alcoholics. *Fortune* magazine estimated the total world drug trade to cost a trillion dollars per year and $100 billion in the United States in 1988.

Together, alcohol and drug abuse treatment account for approximately one-third of all monies spent on all mental illness treatment. On the other hand, total cost, including direct and indirect cost for alcohol and drug abuse, more than doubles the estimated cost for the rest of mental illness. Extraordinary costs are present for some subgroups (e.g., American Indians and Alaskan natives), in which alcohol-related illnesses and injury are three times the rate of the general population; homicide rates for these groups are doubled, and accidents are the second most common cause of death. In addition, liver cirrhosis is high, and fetal alcohol syndrome is 10-fold greater than the general population. The homeless, estimated at numbering 250,000 to 350,000, have a high rate of alcohol-related problems and are susceptible to many health problems (12). More than half of convicted jail inmates have used drugs or alcohol at the time of committing criminal offenses. The awareness of direct and hidden costs of alcoholism and drug abuse to society has led to an increased public consciousness and has made psychoactive substance use disorders a major concern of government and an important economic and political issue as well as public health problem.

## ■ MEDICAL AND PSYCHIATRIC COMPLICATIONS

A complex association of medical and psychiatric problems associated with substance abuse and dependence leading to morbidity and mortality includes the effects of intoxication and overdose, withdrawal, and the complications and consequences of chronic use. All organ systems are affected by alcoholism and drug abuse. The following syndromes are among the major complications: gastritis, ulcers, pancreatitis, liver disease, cardiomyopathy, anemia, neurologic complications, sexual dysfunction, fetal alcohol syndrome, and kidney failure. Increased rates of cancer in the mouth, tongue, larynx, esophagus, and liver have been reported. Liver disease occurs in less than 10 percent of alcoholics; however, more than 11,000 die from liver disease annually (5). Delirium tremens and other withdrawal syndromes can lead to death when accompanied by medical illnesses such as pneumonia, liver failure, subdural hematomas, severe electrolyte imbalances, and diabetes. The use of unsterile needles contributes to the spread of AIDS, hepatitis, skin abscesses, endocarditis, mycotic aneurysms, septic arthritis, osteomyelitis, meningitis, and lung abscesses.

## *FACTORS CONTRIBUTING TO COMPLICATIONS*

Poor self-care, dietary problems, the use of unsterile needles, the admixture of unknown quantities of impure substances, and the psychosocial problems associated with addiction (e.g., the increased personal risk of crime, suicidality, and homicidality) contribute to the medical and dental complications of drug abuse in addition to the effects of the drug itself. The additional use of alcohol can further contribute to liver failure in iv addicts with hepatitis and may lower resistance to infections and increase lung diseases (e.g., pneumonia and tuberculosis). Kidney disease may be caused by antigen-antibody immune complexes resulting from infection and from hypertension, which frequently accompanies substance abuse, especially alcohol and stimulant abuse. Cocaine use may contribute to hypertension, tachycardia, and arrhythmia, and is a cause of sudden death. Patients with combinations of problems (e.g., alcohol withdrawal, diabetes, and hypertension) who are given antidepressants may be especially at high risk for cardiac arrhythmias, vascular problems, and sudden death. Chronic use can reduce sexual performance and desire. Studies indicate that marijuana use decreases serum testosterone in males; the same has been found for chronic use of alcohol. Poor nutrition and vitamin deficiencies contribute to low resistance to illness.

## ■ DENIAL

The patient with substance use disorders may demonstrate denial, dissimulation, and memory problems related to organicity, making it difficult to obtain a clear history. Either because of refusal to cooperate or as a result of being socially isolated, the patient may not have family or friends who can be interviewed. Due to intoxication or overdose, the patient may be unable to answer coherently. Often the patient who is seeking help has been coerced to see the doctor by family, employer, the court, or a family physician, and has mixed feelings about cooperating. In addition to having had a long-term disrespect for authority figures that may have stemmed from being a child of an alcoholic, the patient may have had bad experiences with physicians who were not well informed about substance use problems. The patient needs reassurance that there is reason to be hopeful about the outcome of treatment and an effort needs to be made to reduce blame and guilt. What the patient does not tell the doctor may be as important as what is being told; an alert clinician must watch for observable signs, symptoms, and a mental status characterized by high denial, projection, and rationalization. Laboratory evidence (e.g., urine screens) are often crucial in making a diagnosis and are aids in confronting denial.

## ■ FACILITY PREJUDICES

Mentally ill chemically abusing patients are often inadequately managed in general psychiatric facilities and in freestanding alcohol and drug rehabilitation facilities that are unable to deal with the dual diagnosis. Minimal contact with the psychiatric consultant and primary treatment by alcoholism counselors, who may have insufficient psychiatric training, lead to underdiagnosis and insufficient treatment of additional psychiatric problems. For psychotic patients, an abstinence-oriented program for mentally ill chemically abusing patients is often not as effective in achieving compliance with prescribed psychotropic medications as a general psychiatric unit, unless the need for medication is well explained and accepted. Many psychiatric halfway houses will not accept alcoholics, and halfway houses for substance abusers will frequently not accept patients on medications. Confrontational methods useful in therapeutic communities and self-help groups may be detrimental to those with more severe psychiatric illness. The full-service facilities with psychiatric treatment and rehabilitation are expensive and have problems demonstrating cost effectiveness; however, they represent a healthy eclecticism and provide state-of-the-art treatment in the field.

## ■ REFERENCES

1. Helzer JT: Epidemiology of alcoholism. Consult Clin Psychol 1988; 55:285–292
2. American Psychiatric Association: Diagnostic and Statistical Manual of Mental Disorders, 3rd ed. Washington, DC, American Psychiatric Association, 1980

3. National Institute on Drug Abuse: Drug Use Among American High School Students and Other Young Adults: National Trends Through 1985. Washington, DC, US Department of Health and Human Services, 1986

4. Frances RJ, Allen M: The interaction of substance-use disorders with nonpsychotic psychiatric disorders, in Psychiatry. Edited by Michaels R, Cavenar JO, Brodie HKH, et al. Philadelphia, JB Lippincott Co, 1986

5. Sixth Special Report to the US Congress of Alcohol and Health. Rockville, MD, US Department of Health and Human Services, Public Health Service, January 1987

6. National Household Survey. Rockville, MD, National Institute on Drug Abuse, 1985

7. Washton A, Gold MS, Pottash AC: Intranasal cocaine addiction. Lancet 1984; 2:1374

8. National Institute on Drug Abuse: Client Oriented Data Acquisition Process (CODAP) Annual Data and Quarterly Reports, Statistical Series D and E. Rockville, MD, US Department of Health and Human Services, Alcohol, Drug Abuse, and Mental Health Administration, 1980

9. Health Consequences of Involuntary Smoking: A Report of the Surgeon General. Rockville, MD, US Department of Health and Human Services, 1987

10. Miller JD: National Survey on Drug Abuse: Main Findings, 1982. Rockville, MD, National Institute on Drug Abuse, 1983

11. Niven GR: Alcoholism: a problem in perspective. JAMA 1984; 252:1912–1914

12. Knoll J, Carey K, Hagedorn D, et al: A survey of homeless adults in urban emergency shelters. Hosp Community Psychiatry 1986; 37:283

# 3 DEVELOPMENTAL ISSUES IN THE FIELD

## ■ THE DISEASE CONCEPT

Alcoholism is accepted as a disease by most practitioners and established medical organizations. Definitions can be narrow or broad, culturally defined or changed over time. Disease concepts may focus on the lack of homeostasis, discomfort, difference from the norm, or lack of perfect health. One cannot escape some degree of value judgment in defining disease. Several conditions that previously were defined as diseases have been redefined elsewhere (e.g., masturbation, homosexuality). Thomas Szasz has argued that mental illness is not a medical illness at all but simply a myth that avoids the realization that individuals are not made to be harmonious with their surroundings, and they do not see things the same way society does all the time (1). The new age of neurochemistry, neurotransmitters, receptor systems, and imaging technology, however, has recently developed potentially powerful tools to measure functional abnormalities in the brain. Squaring these two apparently different views of the world is where the controversy surrounds the disease concept of alcoholism.

## HISTORY OF THE DISEASE CONCEPT OF ALCOHOLISM

The concept of the loss of control of alcohol intake can be traced back to the first century A.D. Benjamin Rush and Thomas Trotter introduced the concept of addiction to alcohol in the early 1880s. Magnus Huss first coined the term *alcoholism* in 1849. The temperance movement in this country used strong moralistic arguments that eventually downplayed alcoholism as a disease. Jellinek, the father of the biopsychosocial approach to alcoholism, considered it to be a disease that involves the interaction between alcohol and the biologic and psychological characteristics of the individual with social factors, and described subtypes

(2). In 1956, the American Medical Association recognized alcoholism as a disease. However, drug abuse is often cast in more moralistic terms. Campaigns such as "just say no" may in this sense increase value judgments.

## DEFINING DISEASE

Webster's dictionary defines *disease* as "any departure from health or illness in general: a particular destructive process occurring in an organ or an organism with a specific cause and characteristic pattern" (3). However, few medical problems have a specific cause. Two alternative definitions are as follows. One, disease is the sum of the abnormal phenomena displayed by a group or living organism in association with a specified common characteristic or set of characteristics at which they differ from the norm for their species in such a way as to place them at a biologic disadvantage. Two, when adaption or adjustment fails and the preexisting dynamic steady state is disrupted, then a state of disease may be said to exist until a new balance is restored that may again permit the effective interaction with the environment. Definitions of *syndrome*, *addiction*, *or habit* often overlap periodically with the disease concept.

## ALCOHOLISM AS A DISEASE

Infectious disease is the prototype of medical illnesses. A disease in this sense has a known cause, a characteristic treatment, and known pathophysiology. Alcoholism as a disease shares many of these same principles; however, the insistence by some that alcoholism can be called a disease only if it is based solely on biologic etiology is misguided. Alcoholism is a disease that probably involves several etiologies and has several courses of outcome. This does not conflict with the broad definition of disease. Alcoholism causes morbidity and mortality, has characteristic signs and symptoms, a course, complications, and treatments. Increasing evidence for a strong hereditary predisposition and biologic factors also lends support to the disease concept. The disease concept has been most useful in destigmatizing the behavior from a moralistic realm and in stimulating systematic research into etiology, course, and treatment outcome. Despite the contribution of biologic studies of etiology of psychoactive substance abuse in support of the disease concept, this should not lead to underestimating important cultural, social, situational, ritualistic, developmental, psychological, and cognitive factors. A recent Supreme Court decision ruled that the Veterans Administration (VA) can view alcoholism as "willful misconduct" and consider it not covered as other illnesses would be for purposes of benefits. Although the Supreme Court's decision was not a ruling on the disease concept, it was a setback to those who would like to see a reduction in the stigma of addiction. However, a 1988 congressional omnibus drug bill corrected laws and VA rules to adjust to the disease concept. Increasing public acceptance of the disease concept is reflected in the media and in increasingly enlightened employee assistance programs and company policies encouraging health promotion. Insurance companies have more recently recognized the need for reimbursement for psychoactive substance abuse treatment. However, society has been slow to respond to the provision of adequate numbers and variety of treatment facilities.

## ■ PREVENTION EFFORTS

### *ROLE OF PREVENTION*

With greater scientific advances in understanding of alcoholism and other addictions in terms of description, etiology, pathogenesis, course, and epidemiology, there is an increasing possibility that strategies for prevention may be successful. Advances in genetic understanding of familial alcoholism, for example, may lead to discovery of markers that can identify a high-risk population. However, we are still far from being able to match prevention of infectious disease by vaccination and prevention of parasitic disease by improved sanitary and public health measures. Efforts at border control, increase of public information, and improved efforts at social planning in law enforcement have not led to major changes in the magnitude of the problem. The vast cost of the problem requires greater research to develop a better understanding of the illness, its prevention, and its treatment (4).

## EDUCATIONAL PROGRAMS

Primary prevention efforts have focused heavily on school-based and work-based alcohol education programs and mass media campaigns, along with efforts at limitation of availability of the agent. Programs targeted at students, parents, and employees have significantly increased knowledge regarding alcohol and substance abuse. It is harder to achieve changes in attitudes toward alcohol and drugs, and changes in drinking behavior have been modest or difficult to demonstrate.

Efforts at life-skills training focusing on values clarification abilities, decision making, and drug refusal may be more effective in changing attitudes than cognitive interventions aimed at increasing knowledge alone. Programs that teach young people how to refuse drugs, based on social learning theory, provide information about the hazards of drugs, peer pressure, and means of expanding specific behavioral repertoire for saying no. Through rehearsal of a variety of rejecting responses, it is hoped that at the appropriate situation these responses will be available. These programs often begin at middle school from sixth to ninth grade and use peer leaders to enhance social resistance skills in improved self-management. Discussion, demonstration, and role playing are all techniques that supplement the simple method of "just say no." The factors that increase adolescent abuse include peer pressure, role modeling, desire to obtain adult status, curiosity, low self-esteem, and an unstable family. Drugs may be used to solve painful affects, initiate sexual intimacy, and promote greater group identification. Student assistance model programs include: 1) education and groups, with children of alcoholics especially targeted; 2) treatment or referral for abusing students; 3) early screening of students with behavioral changes; and 4) work with parents and community groups. In one program, 56 percent of the students were self-referred and 73 percent of all students seen were children of alcoholics or drug abusers (5).

Adolescents frequently experiment with alcohol and drug use. A national program of teaching children to refuse substances has been successful only in part. Because of the ubiquitous presence of alcohol in the culture, coming to personal terms with alcohol and substance abuse may represent a developmental task for some teenagers. A "just say no" approach may be most important for those at highest risk for developing an alcohol problem, such as children of alcoholics. Most educational programs touch on myths about alcohol, alcohol advertisement, causes of alcoholism, and the effects of alcohol and drugs on life satisfaction, and also instill positive social skills and behaviors.

## EARLY DETECTION IN ADOLESCENTS

Signs of adolescent drug use include a drop in school performance, irritability, apathy, mood change (including depression), poor self-care, weight loss, oversensitivity with regard to questions about drinking or drugs, and sudden changes in friends. Screening devices in adolescents should include routine medical examinations before camp or in school. The use of urine analysis may help confirm a diagnosis whenever there is reason to raise the question.

## TWELVE-STEP AND OTHER SELF-HELP PROGRAMS

Self-help groups such as Alateen, Alanon, Alcoholics Anonymous, Adult Children of Alcoholics, and Mothers Against Drunk Driving provide support and dissemination of educational materials. Some groups supply important lobbying power. These organizations also help disseminate information and, indirectly through twelve-step work, aid at early case finding and intervention.

## MASS MEDIA

Mass media prevention campaigns on radio, television, and the press use popular peer models as well as messages delivered by prominent sports figures, celebrities, or parental role models (e.g., Nancy Reagan, Rosalyn Carter, and Betty Ford). Polls indicate that an active public service announcement campaign of donated advertising time has been very effective in changing attitudes and challenging myths. This effort in part counters advertisers' use of mass media to increase sales of addictive substances (e.g., alcohol and tobacco). Use and abuse of psychoactive substances are frequently glamorized on television and in films. Commercials treating alcohol positively, with images including camaraderie, relaxation, and enjoyment, contain important subliminal messages; it is not clear what negative impact this advertising has on prevention efforts. Alcohol-containing products such as wine coolers, frequently packaged to look like soft drinks, are sold over the counter in grocery stores and are designed to appeal to a youth market.

## PREVENTION AT THE WORKPLACE

The high loss of employee productivity associated with intoxication and chronic drug abuse can lead to safety hazards, illness, absenteeism, poor work quality, and bad morale. Preemployment drug screens are now being used routinely in the National Football League, in major league baseball, and in hockey leagues. Use of drug screens at the workplace has raised ethical issues such as the individual's right to privacy versus prevention and treatment for the good of a larger group. Olympic athletes are required to give urine samples before events. Abuse of steroids has led to broken dreams and questions about unfair competition. Increasingly, society is demanding use of drug screens, especially in jobs for which hazards produced by impairment are high (e.g., airline pilots, surgeons, transportation workers).

When management and unions work together with employee assistance professionals, confrontation techniques are especially effective. Employees are offered treatment and rehabilitation, with progressive job action taken if the employee continues to have difficulty functioning at work. Additional disciplinary measures can often be avoided if confrontation occurs early enough.

## SOCIAL POLICY AND LEGAL EFFORTS

Greater availability of addictive substances leads to greater craving for them and higher use. Because alcohol and tobacco are widely available, cheap, and legal, they are the most heavily used. Due to the enormous profits that can be gleaned from the sale of drugs, it has proved to be extremely difficult to limit the influx of illegal substances. Illegal drug use is tied to market value, cost, availability, and quality. Limiting availability of alcohol through price manipulation, outward availability, hours of sale, and age restriction policies is one strategy to reduce overall consumption. Forbidding grocery stores from selling distilled alcohol and the banning of hotel room refrigeration dispensers are examples of efforts to reduce exposure of recovering alcoholics and teenagers to marketing pressures that increase availability. Overall rates of liver cirrhosis are correlated with alcohol availability and total alcohol consumption and may be reduced by efforts to limit consumption. The legal drinking age has been raised to 21 throughout the nation, and studies indicate that this has decreased teenage motor vehicle accidents and deaths. Limiting tobacco use in public places has been another controversial measure in an effort to achieve the surgeon general's goal of a "smokeless" society.

## HIGH-RISK GROUPS

Twin, adoption, and half sibling genetic studies and studies of familial versus nonfamilial alcoholism indicate that children of alcoholics are at fourfold higher risk of developing alcoholism (6). Efforts to target programs for those at high risk for heart disease, obesity, hypertension, and cholesterol have been paralleled by programs to assist the high-risk group of children of alcoholics about alternative alcohol-free life-styles. Familial alcoholics have earlier onset of problem drinking, more severe social consequences, less consistently stable family involvement, poor academic and social performance in school, more antisocial behavior, and poorer prognosis in treatment (Table 2).

A major movement has grown up around the problem of being an adult child of an alcoholic. As children, these individuals frequently suffer from stigma, alienation, estrangement, and iso-

TABLE 2. **Characteristics of Familial Alcoholics**

- Earlier onset of problem drinking
- More severe social consequences
- Less consistently stable family involvement
- Poor academic and social performance in school
- More antisocial behavior
- Poorer prognosis in treatment

lation. Their parents are frequently inconsistent and emotionally depriving, force them into inappropriate roles, are more likely to be aggressive or sexually abusing, or are more likely to have difficult divorces and may abandon their children. Struggling with feelings of anger, confusion, and helplessness, these children tend to distrust authority figures, depend more on peers, and pick friends from similarly troubled families. This is likely to lead to a distrust of doctors, nurses, and other health care professionals. The peer group grows up protesting their parents' behavior, trying to be different, but ending up with the same problems. This may explain why self-help groups, group therapy, and family approaches that take into account peer support are so successful.

## RELATIONSHIP TO OTHER PREVENTION EFFORTS

Early treatment of an alcohol or drug problem may also help prevent development of other problems, such as depression or antisocial personality. Similarly, early treatment of depression, attention deficit hyperactivity disorder, or anxiety disorders may help to prevent the development of an alcohol or drug problem, and thereby progression to antisocial personality. These illnesses have complicated interactions and each can precede, contribute to, or coexist with the other.

## ■ CLINICAL IMPLICATIONS OF RESEARCH FINDINGS

### FAMILIAL STUDIES AND HIGH-RISK POPULATIONS

Many lines of research have focused in on a search for biologic markers of alcohol and substance abuse. Clinically, this research has helped increase the awareness of the complexity of etiology of these disorders. Forty years ago, Jellinek and Jolliffee began to describe a familial form of alcoholism. Researchers in the past decade began to confirm a familial type of alcoholism that has an earlier onset, greater severity, and poorer outcome. Although genetic influences in alcoholism have become fairly well established through twin, adoption, and split sibling studies, the mode of transmission is not clear.

## BIOLOGIC MARKERS

Biologic markers are associated findings, if not causal findings, that may help us to 1) identify high-risk individuals before the onset of abuse, 2) identify dependence when it does exist, and 3) follow the course of the disease.

Identifying children at high risk for alcoholism or substance abuse has been one major research thrust. Schuckit has been working on multiple markers in biologic sons of alcoholics (7) (Table 3). These findings have included positive findings of decreased subjective feelings of intoxication in not-yet-alcoholic children of alcoholics and of less impairment of motor performance. He has also reported less body sway or static ataxia with alcohol challenge and less change in cortisol and prolactin levels when compared to controls. Schuckit has been attempting to use these multiple markers to increase their predictive value. This research needs more replication. However, the clinician who is working in adolescent or young adult populations especially should focus closely on the patient's initial experiences with alcohol. Does the adolescent drink much more than peers and not show signs or symptoms of intoxication? What is the best advice for a young person who drinks, has little adverse effects in the beginning, but has a strong family history of dependence? An early choice of abstinence may be the safest form of prevention for these individuals. Often these teenagers will describe their first real experience with alcohol as a revelation, an "ah ha"

TABLE 3. **Possible Markers of Alcoholism in Biologic Sons of Alcoholics**

- Decreased subjective feelings of intoxication
- Less impairment of motor performance
- Less body sway
- Less static ataxia
- Less change in cortisol and prolactin levels
- Low P3 amplitude (electroencephalogram)
- Increased alpha wave activity

experience in which alcohol is accepted as a way to handle anxiety, decrease stress, and express emotions.

## ELECTROENCEPHALOGRAPHIC MARKERS

Begleiter and Porjesz have been looking at auditory brainstem potentials in abstinent alcoholics and sons of alcoholics (8). Abstinent alcoholics demonstrate a low amplitude P3 component when compared to controls. The P3 component may be related to motivational properties of stimuli and may be involved in the process of memory. Low P3 amplitude has also been found in sons of alcoholics. Although specificity of this possible marker is not high enough for predictive value, this is a promising area of research. Increased alpha wave activity with alcohol exposure in alcoholics versus controls has also been reported (Table 3).

## CELLULAR MECHANISMS

Another line of research has been looking at clues at the cellular level. Various cellular membranes have been studied in alcohol-consuming animals and alcoholic patients. Although cellular membranes become more fluid with acute exposure of alcohol, in chronic alcoholics they become more rigid and demonstrate less fluidity with reexposure (9). This kind of study may point to a marker that serves as an ancillary test in diagnosis. Another line of research on the cellular level has been the difference in platelet enzyme activity between alcoholics and nonalcoholics. Platelet monoamine oxidase (MAO) has been found to be lower in alcoholics and their first-degree relatives when compared to controls. This finding however, is probably nonspecific.

More recently, Tabakoff et al. reported a significantly higher inhibition of MAO in alcoholics with alcohol challenge (10). Discriminant analysis showed that inhibition of MAO correctly classified 75 percent of the alcoholics and 73 percent of the controls. Again, this kind of research may help clinicians better identify problem drinkers. Being able to show laboratory evidence to potential problem drinkers may have some influence on subsequent behavior.

Other promising areas of research have been markers of decreased epinephrine responsiveness and epinephrine turnover, research on gamma-aminobutyric acid (GABA)-operated calcium channels, and calcium-induced electrophysiologic effects. Prospective longitudinal study of sons of alcoholics have reported some evidence of poor neuropsychological performance in areas such as categorizing ability, organization, planning, abstracting, and problem-solving ability. Tarter et al. suggested that minimal brain dysfunction or conduct disorder may predispose toward alcoholism and may be an expression of an underlying inherited temperament (11).

## ■ REFERENCES

1. Szasz T: The Myth of Mental Illness: Foundations of a Theory of Personal Conduct. New York, Harper, 1961
2. Jellinek EM: The Disease Concept of Alcoholism. New Haven, CT, Hillhouse Press, 1960
3. Webster's New Collegiate Dictionary. Springfield, MA, G & C Merriam Co, 1976
4. Frances RJ, Franklin JE: Primary prevention of alcoholism and drug abuse, in Primary Prevention in Psychiatry. Edited by Talbott S, Barter J. Washington, DC, American Psychiatric Press, 1987, pp 153–184
5. Chambers J, Morehouse E: A cooperative model for preventing alcohol and drug abuse. NASSP Bulletin, January, 1983
6. Goodwin DW: Alcoholism and genetics. Arch Gen Psychiatry 42:171–174, 1985
7. Schuckit MA: Biological Vulnerability to Alcoholism. Consult Clin Psychol 1987; 55:301–309
8. Begleiter H, Porjesz B: Potential biological markers in individuals at high risk for developing alcoholism. Alcoholism: Clinical and Experimental Research 1988; 3:488–493
9 Wood WG, Lahiri S, Gorka C, et al: In vitro effects of ethanol on erythrocyte membrane fluidity of alcoholic patients: an electron spin resonance study. Alcoholism: Clinical and Experimental Research 1987; 11:37–41
10. Tabakoff B, Hoffman PL, Lee JM, et al: Differences in platelet enzyme activity between alcoholics and nonalcoholics. N Engl J Med 1988; 318:134–139
11. Tarter RE, Edwards K: Psychological factors associated with the risk for alcoholism. Alcoholism: Clinical and Experimental Research 1988; 12(4)

# DEFINITIONS AND DIAGNOSIS    4

■ **PSYCHOACTIVE SUBSTANCE ABUSE**

There has been an evolution of nomenclature regarding psychoactive substances that has resulted from advances in understanding biologic and psychosocial aspects of chemical abuse and dependency. This includes development of specific behavioral criteria that are amenable to studying worldwide public health problems through use of instruments for measuring agreed-on criteria for diagnosis of levels of severity of psychoactive substance use disorders. The challenge has been to develop a nomenclature that is consistent across cultures and across substances that validly describes the clinical phenomena. The Diagnostic and Statistical Manual of Mental Disorders (DSM-III) (1) attempted to operationalize criteria for diagnosis to develop research instruments for measuring substance abuse and dependence across populations. A major advance was the ability to classify substance use disorders along with other Axis I, II, and III disorders to allow for greater awareness of the existence and the interaction of multiple diagnoses. DSM-III introduced the term *substance abuse* as a pattern of pathologic use of at least one month's duration that leads to impairment in social or occupational functioning. *Substance dependence* was defined as requiring the presence of tolerance or withdrawal symptoms.

DSM-III-R (2) introduced the term *psychoactive* to differentiate psychoactive substance abuse and dependence from nutritional or other adverse drug-related problems. Table 4 lists the classes of substances. The concept of dependence is broadened in DSM-III-R to include at least three significant behaviors out of a nine-item, polythetic scheme that includes psychosocial problems indicating a major problem with a psychoactive substance (Table 5). Patterns of tolerance and withdrawal, still listed as criteria, are no longer the only criteria for dependence. Most patients who would have been labeled abusers in DSM-III are called dependent in DSM-III-R. The severity of dependence can be indexed as mild, moderate, severe, in partial remission, or in full remission (Table 6).

TABLE 4.  **DSM-III-R Psychoactive Substance Abuse Disorders**

| | |
|---|---|
| 305.00 | Alcohol abuse |
| 305.40 | Sedative, hypnotic, or anxiolytic abuse |
| 305.50 | Opioid abuse |
| 305.60 | Cocaine abuse |
| 305.70 | Amphetamine or similarly acting sympathomimetic abuse |
| 305.90 | Phencyclidine (PCP) or similarly acting arylcyclohexylamine abuse |
| 305.30 | Hallucinogen abuse |
| 305.20 | Cannabis abuse |
| 305.90 | Inhalant abuse |
| 305.90 | Polysubstance abuse |
| 305.90 | Psychoactive substance abuse NOS |

*Note.* Adapted with permission from the *Diagnostic and Statistical Manual of Mental Disorders,* Third Edition, Revised. Copyright © 1987 American Psychiatric Association.

Psychoactive substance abuse is narrowed in DSM-III-R to those who continue substance use despite significant problems caused by the use in those who do not meet criteria for psychoactive substance dependency (Table 7). The problem of delineating at which set points risk factors (hazardous use), abuse (harmful use), and dependence develop in the course of illness has accompanied considerable controversy regarding what level of problem or risk factor should constitute a disorder. Tolerance and withdrawal are dimensional rather than categorical phenomena, and significant psychosocial problems contribute to the severity of morbidity and mortality.

## EVOLVING DEFINITIONS

The World Health Organization (WHO) has been working toward developing the International Classification of Diseases, 10th edition (ICD-10), scheduled to appear in 1993. They will probably use the DSM-III-R term *psychoactive*. However, they

TABLE 5. **DSM-III-R Diagnostic Criteria for Psychoactive Substance Dependence**

---

A. At least three of the following:

(1) substance often taken in larger amounts or over a longer period than the person intended

(2) persistent desire or one or more unsuccessful efforts to cut down or control substance use

(3) a great deal of time spent in activities necessary to get the substance (e.g., theft), taking the substance (e.g., chain smoking), or recovering from its effects

(4) frequent intoxication or withdrawal symptoms when expected to fulfill major role obligations at work, school, at home (e.g., does not go to work because hung over, goes to school or work "high," intoxicated while taking care of his or her children), or when substance use is physically hazardous (e.g., drives when intoxicated)

(5) important social, occupational, or recreational activities given up or reduced because of substance use

(6) continued substance use despite knowledge of having a persistent or recurrent social, psychological, or physical problem that is caused or exacerbated by the use of the substance (e.g., keeps using heroin despite family arguments about it, cocaine-induced depression, or having an ulcer made worse by drinking)

(7) marked tolerance: need for markedly increased amounts of the substance (i.e., at least a 50% increase) in order to achieve intoxication or desired effect, or markedly diminished effect with continued use of the same amount

**Note:** The following items may not apply to cannabis, hallucinogens, or phencyclidine (PCP):

(8) characteristic withdrawal symptoms (see specific withdrawal syndromes under Psychoactive Substance-induced Organic Mental Disorders)

(9) substance often taken to relieve or avoid withdrawal symptoms

B. Some symptoms of the disturbance have persisted for at least one month, or have occurred repeatedly over a longer period of time.

---

*Note.* Adapted with permission from the *Diagnostic and Statistical Manual of Mental Disorders,* Third Edition, Revised. Copyright © 1987 American Psychiatric Association.

**TABLE 6. DSM-III-R Criteria for Severity of Psychoactive Substance Dependence**

**Mild:** Few, if any, symptoms in excess of those required to make the diagnosis, and the symptoms result in no more than mild impairment in occupational functioning or in usual social activities or relationships with others.

**Moderate:** Symptoms or functional impairment between "mild" and "severe."

**Severe:** Many symptoms in excess of those required to make the diagnosis, and symptoms markedly interfere with occupational functioning or with usual social activities or relationships with others.

**In Partial Remission:** During the past six months, some use of the substance and some symptoms of dependence.

**In Full Remission:** During the past six months, either no use of the substance, or use of the substance and no symptoms of dependence.

*Note.* Adapted with permission from the *Diagnostic and Statistical Manual of Mental Disorders,* Third Edition, Revised. Copyright © 1987 American Psychiatric Association.

**TABLE 7. DSM-III-R Diagnostic Criteria for Psychoactive Substance Abuse**

A. A maladaptive pattern of psychoactive substance use indicated by at least one of the following:

   (1) continued use despite knowledge of having a persistent or recurrent social, occupational, psychological, or physical problem that is caused or exacerbated by use of the psychoactive substance

   (2) recurrent use in situations in which use is physically hazardous (e.g., driving while intoxicated)

B. Some symptoms of the disturbance have persisted for at least one month, or have occurred repeatedly over a longer period of time.

C. Never met the criteria for Psychoactive Substance Dependence for this substance.

*Note.* Adapted with permission from the *Diagnostic and Statistical Manual of Mental Disorders,* Third Edition, Revised. Copyright © 1987 American Psychiatric Association.

are likely to include a greater spectrum of problems, such as hazardous and harmful use. This may be viewed as relevant to prevention and early detection of potential problems compared with DSM-III-R, in which risk factors are clearly differentiated from disorders.

Work is in progress for DSM-IV, to be completed by 1993. Possible areas for change in the DSM-IV include greater attention to etiologic factors such as familial and genetic predisposition; more rigorous, well-defined criteria; greater awareness of the interaction of primary, secondary, and concomitant additional psychiatric disorders; and possibly a clearer definition of psychoactive substance-induced acute and chronic personality effects. Greater clarification of risk factors for psychoactive substance abuse, attention to early diagnosis, and clearer descriptions of withdrawal effects (especially of cocaine and benzodiazepines) may also be included. Concepts regarding a general drug dependence syndrome, which is achieving wide acceptance, are likely to continue to undergo gradual change.

## ■ ORGANIC MENTAL DISORDERS

Organic mental disorders associated with psychoactive substances have been grouped with other disorders involving psychoactive substances and DSM-III-R. Organic disorders that include cannabis delirium, cocaine withdrawal, cocaine delirium, and cocaine delusional disorder have been introduced in DSM-III-R. A number of drugs that formerly did not have the diagnosis of dependence (e.g., cocaine, phencyclidine, hallucinogens, and inhalants) are now included. The term *sedative, hypnotic, or anxiolytic* has replaced *barbiturate and similarly acting sedative or hypnotic.*

A new organic flashback syndrome that is caused by phencyclidine and hallucinogens is defined as the reexperiencing of one or more of the perceptual symptoms that the patient had experienced while intoxicated (e.g., hallucinations or derealization that result in marked distress).

## ■ ALCOHOL

### *ALCOHOL DEPENDENCE AND ABUSE*

The DSM-III-R diagnostic criteria for alcohol dependence and abuse follows those for other substance disorders as described in Tables 5, 6, and 7. Major tolerance to alcohol is noted when a 180-pound man, for example, can consume five drinks in an hour and does not develop signs of intoxication. Use of a quart of vodka, a gallon of wine, or a case of beer per day or findings of blood alcohol levels (BAL) over 0.15 mg percent also demonstrate tolerance and are likely indicators of alcoholism. Alcohol withdrawal generally begins within several hours of stopping extended, heavy drinking and is diagnosed by coarse tremors of hands, tongue, and eyelids, occurring with at least one of the following: nausea or vomiting; malaise or weakness; autonomic hypersensitivity; anxiety, depressed mood, or irritability; transient hallucinations or illusions; or headache. Loss of control of drinking is evidenced when a person may decide to take only one drink of alcohol, but after taking this first drink continues to drink until severely intoxicated. Attempts to reduce excessive drinking may be evidenced by eliminating alcohol at home or switching to wine or beer, and then beginning to hide alcohol around the house. The choice of retirement to have adequate time and space to drink may indicate alcohol is becoming a preoccupation. Examples of use of alcohol when a person is expected to fulfill major social obligations are a physician's drinking before returning to the hospital to see patients or anyone drinking when driving. Also helpful in making the diagnosis is the development of medical and psychiatric complications related to alcohol use. Alcohol dependence tends to occur in families, and there is a pattern of genetic influence in the transmission of this disorder.

### *ALCOHOL INTOXICATION*

The most frequent alcohol-induced organic mental disorder, alcohol intoxication, is time-limited, with onset of intoxication depending on tolerance, amount ingested, and amount absorbed over time. It is affected by interactions with other drugs and medications used and by individual variation. Intoxication stages range from mild inebriation to anesthesia, coma, respiratory depression, and early death. In low doses, alcohol may produce clinical excitement. With increasing blood levels, and relative to degree of tolerance, alcohol can lead to euphoria, mild coordination problems, ataxia, confusion, and decreased consciousness, and then to anesthesia, coma, and death, with BALs greater than 0.4 mg percent. Chronic heavy drinkers maintain high BALs at lower stages of effect. Alcohol impairs motor performance and muscular control; leads to slurred speech, flushed face, ataxia, slower thinking; and leads to poor concentration, reasoning, attention, and ability to form word associations. Alcohol intoxication may affect heart rate, nystagmus and electroencephalogram (EEG) readings; may slow reaction times; and may cause behavioral changes, including mood lability, impaired judgment, impaired social or occupational functioning, cognitive problems, and disinhibition of sexual or aggressive impulses.

Alcohol intoxication increases disinhibition, which potentiates suicidal and homicidal behavior. Alcohol intoxication also increases risk-taking behaviors, including those that may lead to spread of human immunodeficiency virus (HIV) infection. While alcohol intoxication contributes to maladaptive behavior (e.g., impaired judgment and irritability), alcohol use without intoxication may produce some changes that are generally not harmful (e.g., increased sociability and loquacity). Intoxication with alcohol closely resembles intoxication due to sedatives, hypnotics, and anxiolytics. It should be noted that the odor of alcohol does not rule out the possibility that more than one substance is used.

### DIFFERENTIAL DIAGNOSIS OF ALCOHOL INTOXICATION

Other neurologic diseases such as cerebellar ataxias from multiple sclerosis may also mimic some of the physiologic signs and symptoms of alcohol intoxication. Alcohol idiosyncratic intoxication, which is described below, follows ingestion of doses of alcohol that would be too low to cause intoxication in most people (Table 8).

## ALCOHOL IDIOSYNCRATIC INTOXICATION

The principal feature of alcohol idiosyncratic intoxication is a major behavioral change usually related to aggression with

TABLE 8. **Pathologic Neuropsychiatric Signs and Symptoms of Alcohol-Induced Organic Mental Disorders**

| Syndrome | Key Neuro-psychiatric Signs and Symptoms | Time of Onset | Treatment (Medication) |
|---|---|---|---|
| Alcohol intoxication | Acute organic brain syndrome | Rapid, depends on tolerance of individual | Time, protective environment |
| Alcohol withdrawal | Transient sensory disturbances possible | Several hours; symptoms 24 to 48 hours after last drink or relative drop in level | See Table 20 |
| Alcohol seizures | Loss of consciousness, tonic-clonic movements, urinary incontinence, post-ictal confusion; look for focal signs | Seven to 38 hours after cessation of alcohol use | Diazepam, phenytoin; maintenance phenytoin if underlying seizure disorder is present; chlordiazepoxide detox |
| Alcohol withdrawal delirium | Marked variations in levels of consciousness and dis-orientation, may be fatal | Gradual onset two to three days after cessation of alcohol; peak intensity at four to five days | Chlordiazepoxide; haloperidol 2 to 5 mg po bid for psychotic symptomatology may be added if necessary |
| Alcohol hallucinosis | Clear sensorium, auditory hallucinations | Usually within 48 hours of last use | Haloperidol 2 to 5 mg po bid for psychotic symptoms |

TABLE 8. **Pathologic Neuropsychiatric Signs and Symptoms of Alcohol-Induced Organic Mental Disorders** *(cont)*

| Syndrome | Key Neuro-psychiatric Signs and Symptoms | Time of Onset | Treatment (Medication) |
|---|---|---|---|
| Wernicke's encephalopathy | Mental confusion, ataxia | Abrupt onset; ataxia may precede mental confusion | Thiamine 100 mg iv with MgSO₄ 1 to 2 ml in 50 percent solution should be given prior to glucose loading |

*Note.* Adapted from Frances RJ, Franklin JE Jr: Alcohol-Induced Organic Mental Disorders, in *The American Psychiatric Press Textbook of Neuropsychiatry.* Edited by Hales RE, Yudofsky SC. Washington, DC, American Psychiatric Press, 1987. Copyright © 1987 American Psychiatric Press.

blind, unfocused, and assaultive behavior, usually accompanied by subsequent amnesia for the period of intoxication, in patients with recent ingestion of an amount of alcohol insufficient to induce intoxication in most people. There is a marked behavioral change, atypical of the personality of the individual and occurring rapidly after mild alcohol intake. Some patients with this problem have had temporal lobe spikes on EEG after small amounts of alcohol. It is possible that this condition is related to brain injury, trauma, and encephalitis, and other debilitating physical illnesses. Advancing age may also be associated with reduced tolerance to alcohol. This condition needs to be distinguished from temporal lobe epilepsy, use of other substances, and malingering.

## BLACKOUTS

Blackouts are periods of amnesia for events and behavior during periods of intoxication even though the state of consciousness may not be abnormal when observed by others. They may occur in nonalcoholics in episodes of heavy drinking as well as at any time in the progression of the disease of alcoholism. They may also occur with barbiturate intoxication. Severity and duration of alcoholism correlate with the occurrence of blackouts.

## ALCOHOL AMNESTIC DISORDER

Alcohol amnestic syndrome, also known as Korsakoff's syndrome, is caused by vitamin deficiency associated with prolonged heavy ingestion of alcohol. It is associated with neurologic disturbances such as peripheral neuropathy, cerebellar ataxia, and myopathy. It often follows an acute episode of Wernicke's encephalopathy, which is marked by confusion, ataxia, eye-movement abnormalities, and other neurologic signs. After these manifestations subside, a severe impairment of memory, the alcohol amnestic disorder, remains and is marked by the presence of confabulation. Early treatment of Wernicke's disease with large doses of thiamine may prevent the development of alcohol amnestic disorder.

## DEMENTIA ASSOCIATED WITH ALCOHOLISM

Prolonged and heavy use of alcohol may be followed by the development of a dementia. Diagnosis is confirmed by waiting at least three weeks after withdrawal of alcohol. Dementia usually occurs after many years of heavy drinking and generally appears after age 35. With the dementia, there is always impairment of social and occupational functioning, which may, when serious, lead to care in a nursing home facility. The cognitive impairment is broader than the sphere of memory alone, which occurs in alcohol amnestic disorder, and has no other etiology than alcohol use.

## ALCOHOL HALLUCINOSIS

This organic hallucinosis is marked by vivid and persistent hallucinations occurring usually within 48 hours after stopping or reducing drinking in alcohol-dependent individuals. Both auditory and visual hallucinations can occur. The hallucinations can consist of hissing or buzzing, but are usually voices that are unpleasant and disturbing and may address the person directly or more likely speak in the third person. The hallucinations occur in a clear sensorium with lower amounts of autonomic symptoms than in delirium tremens. They usually occur after age 40 and after more than 10 years of heavy drinking. This disorder may last several weeks or months. The person may be extremely frightened and respond to the hallucinations as though they were real. This can lead to self-destructive or aggressive behavior.

## UNCOMPLICATED ALCOHOL WITHDRAWAL

A relative drop in the BAL can precipitate alcohol withdrawal symptoms even during continuous alcohol consumption. Binge patterns and long-term alcoholism increase withdrawal phenomena. Central features of the disorder include coarse tremor of hands, tongue, or eyelids; nausea or vomiting; malaise or weakness; autonomic hyperactivity (i.e., tachycardia, sweating, and elevated blood pressure); anxiety, depressed mood, or irritability; transient hallucinations (generally poorly formed) or illusions; headache; and insomnia. Peak symptoms occur 24 to 48 hours after the last drink and subside in five to seven days even without treatment. Insomnia and irritability may last 10 days or longer. The withdrawal symptoms may precipitate a relapse. Complications of major motor seizures ("rum fits") occur and are more likely to develop in those with a history of epilepsy and in those with other physical illnesses, malnutrition, fatigue, and depression.

## ALCOHOL WITHDRAWAL SEIZURES

Alcohol withdrawal seizures generally occur seven to 38 hours after the last alcohol use in chronic drinkers, peaking at approximately 24 hours. Intoxication with alcohol lowers seizure threshold. Hypomagnesemia, respiratory alkylosis, hypoglycemia, and increased intracellular sodium also tend to be associated with alcohol withdrawal seizures.

## ALCOHOL WITHDRAWAL DELIRIUM (DELIRIUM TREMENS)

Delirium tremens develops after recent reduction or cessation of heavy alcohol use, usually within a week, and is marked by tachycardia and sweating. The hallucinations may be visual, auditory, or tactile and are generally vivid, with frequent reports of insects, small animals, or other perceptual distortions along with terror and agitation. In addition, there are delusions, agitation, insomnia, mild fever, and marked autonomic arousal, which can occur suddenly and develop two to three days after heavy drinking, usually reaching a peak intensity on the fourth or fifth day. There is confusion, disorientation, fluctuating or clouding consciousness, and perceptual disturbances in addition to the usual withdrawal features. It occurs usually five to 15 years after onset of heavy drinking and in individuals with concomitant physical illness and poor social supports. It is associated with infections, subdural hematomas, trauma, liver disease, and metabolic disorders. The cause of death is usually infectious fat emboli, or cardiac arrhythmias, which are usually associated with hyperkalemia, hyperpyrexia, and poor hydration.

## ■ SEDATIVES, HYPNOTICS, AND ANXIOLYTICS

Hypnotics are generally used for sedation and as sleep medications and include benzodiazepines (e.g., flurazepam, triazolam, temazepam) and other substances unrelated to benzodiazepines (e.g., ethchlorvynol, glutethimide, chloral hydrate, methaqualone, and the barbiturates). The diagnosis of sedative abuse may be complicated because it is often iatrogenic in the context of treatment for sleep, anxiety, or medical disorders. Polysubstance abusers frequently self-medicate with sedatives to treat the undesirable, agitating effects of cocaine or amphetamine. Definitions for this class and other classes of drugs follow the definitions of abuse and dependence presented in Tables 5, 6, and 7. Degree of physical dependence is dose- and time-related. Tolerance to barbiturates may develop rapidly. Intoxication, withdrawal delirium, and amnestic disorder symptoms parallel those found with alcoholism. However, due to a longer half-life, withdrawal from some benzodiazepines may not be evident until seven to 10 days after cessation. In addition, withdrawal is frequently more severe and seizures are more common. It is important to distinguish legitimate use of these medications from neuroadaption and maladaptive habituation (even when prescribed by a physician) and from illegal use.

# ■ OPIOIDS

Opioids include natural opioids (e.g., heroin and morphine) and synthetics with morphine-like action (e.g., codeine, hydromorphone, meperidine, methadone, and oxycodone). Opioids act on opiate receptors and are generally prescribed as analgesics, anesthetics, or cough suppressants. Pentazocine and buprenorphine have both direct opioid agonist effects and antagonist effects. Opioids may be in pill form, but may also be used iv. Heroin is usually used iv, but may also be smoked or nasally inhaled. High levels of tolerance occur with chronic use. Abuse of opioids may begin with prescriptions for legitimate treatment of chronic pain or cough suppression, with neuroadaptation and escalation of dosage, self-medication, and drug-seeking behavior. Another more frequent pattern that leads to dependence occurs in teenagers and young adults with opioids purchased illegally to reach euphoria, or frequently combined with cocaine and other substances to maximize a "high" and take the edge off unpleasant side effects. The use of opioids is frequently preceded by use of other drugs in young people. Continuation of other drug abuse is frequent after a pattern has been established. The DSM-III-R definition of opioid dependence and abuse is similar to other substances (Tables 5 and 6).

## *OPIOID-INDUCED INTOXICATION*

Behavioral changes from iv opioids rapidly begin two to five minutes after use, with euphoria lasting 10 to 30 minutes. A two- to six-hour period of lethargy, sleep, apathy, or dysphoria, along with impaired judgment and impaired occupational functioning occurs. Aggression and violence are rarely associated with opioid intoxication, although not uncommon among those with drug-seeking behavior and withdrawal. Intoxication is marked by pupillary constriction or, in severe overdoses, by dilation due to anoxia. Drowsiness, slurred speech, and impairment in attention and memory are other signs.

Accidental opioid overdose manifested with coma, shock, and pinpoint pupils (or dilation in severe cases) and depressed respiration may progress to death. Diagnosis and rapid action is crucial because use of naloxone, a narcotic antagonist, rapidly reverses the syndrome. Opioid intoxication is distinguished from alcohol and sedative intoxication by presence of pupillary constriction and by toxicologic report.

## OPIOID WITHDRAWAL

Recent reduction or cessation of opioid use leads to lacrimation, rhinorrhea, pupillary dilation, piloerection, sweating, diarrhea, yawning, mild hypertension, tachycardia, fever, and insomnia. Withdrawal may be precipitated by use of a narcotic antagonist and generally occurs after one to two weeks of continuous opioid use. Additional symptoms include restlessness, irritability, depression, tremor, weakness, nausea, vomiting, and muscle and joint pains. A general flu-like syndrome is accompanied by complaints, demands, and drug-seeking behavior. The syndrome generally begins within six to eight hours of last dose and peaks in 48 to 72 hours; the greatest physical withdrawal disappears in seven to 10 days. The onset of withdrawal depends on half-life of the opioid, with methadone withdrawal, one to three days, having a later onset than meperidine, which may peak within eight to 12 hours and last 10 to 14 days. Although intensely felt, opioid withdrawal is generally not life-threatening unless there is an additional severe physical disorder such as heart disease (3).

## ■ COCAINE

A variety of cocaine preparations and forms of administration are available, including coca leaves (chewed), coca paste (smoked), cocaine hydrochloride powder (inhaled or injected), and cocaine alkaloid, "free-base," or "crack" (smoked). The smokeable and iv forms of cocaine increase the rapidity and intensity of the euphoric effects and addictive potential, with intoxication occurring seconds after inhalation. "Speed balling," mixing cocaine and heroin, is particularly dangerous due to potentiation of respiratory depressant effects. "Crack" is cocaine alkaloid that is extracted from hydrochloride salt through use of sodium bicarbonate or ether. The resulting "free-base" has a low melting point and can therefore be changed into gas and smoked.

Cocaine may be used episodically or chronically and in endless episodes of bingeing, with periods of continuous high-dose use.

## COCAINE INTOXICATION

Cocaine intoxication is marked by euphoria, fighting, grandiosity, hypervigilence, psychomotor agitation, impaired judgment, and impaired social or occupational functioning. Other signs include tachycardia, pupillary dilation, elevated blood pressure, perspiration or chills, nausea and vomiting, and visual or tactile hallucinations. These usually begin within one hour after administration and, with inhalation, may occur within a few seconds. There may be confused speech, anxiety, apprehension, headache, ideas of reference, paranoid ideation, increased sexual interest, ringing in the ears, formication (the sensation of insects creeping on one's skin), or visual hallucinations. After the immediate effects of the "high," a crash may occur, including dysphoric moods, depression, anxiety, craving for cocaine, and feelings of fatigue and irritability. Beyond 24 hours, the crash becomes cocaine withdrawal. Intoxication does not usually last long. Full recovery usually occurs within 48 hours. The clinical picture is similar to amphetamine intoxication and phencyclidine intoxication, with toxicology needed to determine diagnosis.

## COCAINE WITHDRAWAL

Cocaine withdrawal is accompanied by dysphoric mood with depression, irritability, anxiety, fatigue, insomnia or hyposomnia, and psychomotor agitation. Withdrawal occurs more than 24 hours after cessation of last use. Withdrawal generally peaks in two to four days, although irritability and depression may continue for months.

## COCAINE DELIRIUM

Delirium may occur within 24 hours of cocaine use and depends on confirmation by toxicology with occasional presence of tactile and olfactory hallucinations. Violent or aggressive behavior is frequent and may require restraint. Delirium is self-limited and usually resolves after six hours.

## COCAINE DELUSIONAL DISORDER

An organic delusional syndrome resulting from cocaine use is marked by rapidly developing persecutory delusions, which may be accompanied by distortion of body image and misperception of people's faces and may cause aggressive or violent action. It may also be accompanied by formication.

## ■ AMPHETAMINES

Amphetamines, or similarly acting sympathomimetic abuse and dependency, is in many ways similar to the effects of cocaine. Dextroamphetamine (Dexedrine) and methylphenidate (Ritalin) used for the treatment of narcolepsy and attention deficit hyperactivity disorders have been diverted and abused. Signs and symptoms of amphetamine use parallel those of cocaine abuse and dependence. Amphetamine psychosis can resemble acute paranoid schizophrenia, with a frequent feature of visual hallucinations. Patterns of use include oral administration in pill form predominating and resemble cocaine with binge episodes alternating with crash symptoms. Use of amphetamines iv produces a rapid euphoria similar to cocaine use. Effects of amphetamines may last longer than cocaine. Peripheral sympathomimetic effects may be more potent.

Intoxication (Table 9), withdrawal, delirium, and delusional disorders are similar to those described above for cocaine.

## ■ PHENCYCLIDINE

Phencyclidine (PCP) is an anesthetic that was initially used for animal surgery and has become a street drug with epidemic use in certain eastern urban areas. Other variations of PCP include ketamine (ketalar) and the thiophene analogue of phencyclidine (TCP). These substances can be used orally or iv and can be smoked and inhaled. PCP is also sold under the names "angel dust" and "PeaCe" pill. PCP is often mixed with other substances such as amphetamines, cannabis, cocaine, or hallucinogens. Dependence may have a rapid onset, and effects are generally unpredictable. Intoxication begins within five minutes, peaks in 30 minutes, and is accompanied by affective instability

TABLE 9. **DSM-III-R Diagnostic Criteria for Amphetamine or Similarly Acting Sympathomimetic Intoxication**

A. Recent use of amphetamine or a similarly acting sympathomimetic.

B. Maladaptive behavioral changes, e.g., fighting, grandiosity, hypervigilance, psychomotor agitation, impaired judgment, impaired social or occupational functioning.

C. At least two of the following signs within one hour of use:
   (1) tachycardia
   (2) pupillary dilation
   (3) elevated blood pressure
   (4) perspiration or chills
   (5) nausea or vomiting

D. Not due to any physical or other mental disorder.

*Note.* Reprinted with permission from the *Diagnostic and Statistical Manual of Mental Disorders.* Third Edition, Revised. Copyright © 1987 American Psychiatric Association.

with a range from euphoria to anxiety, stereotypical repetitive behavior, and bizarre aggressive behavior. Distorted perceptions, numbness, and confusion are also common. Violent murders may also occur during PCP use. Physical signs include high blood pressure, muscular rigidity, ataxia, and, at high dosages, hyperthermia, involuntary movements, and coma. Dilated pupils and nystagmus, particularly vertical nystagmus, is characteristic of PCP use and helps confirm the diagnosis. It is also important to get toxicologic confirmation. Chronic psychotic episodes may also occur, along with long-term neuropsychological deficits. PCP may also induce organic mental disorders such as intoxication and delirium. The diagnosis of psychoactive substance dependence for PCP includes the first seven items on Table 5. Items 8 and 9 may not apply because of lack of establishment of a clear-cut withdrawal pattern.

## ■ HALLUCINOGENS

Hallucinogens have hallucinogenic properties and are structurally related to 5-hydroxytryptamine, lysergic acid diethylamide (LSD), and dimethyl tryptamine (DMT) and substances related to catecholamine (mescaline). Experimental use with psychedelics was most common in the 1960s and 1970s and may be increasing in some areas among young people. Use of psychedelics more than 20 times is considered to be chronic abuse. Hallucinogen dependence is defined in Table 5, and a withdrawal pattern is usually not found. Hallucinogen intoxication with LSD and related drugs leads to perceptual changes and is affected by set and setting. Use of these substances impairs normal cognitive and perceptual functions.

## HALLUCINOGEN HALLUCINOSIS

Organic effects of the drug include hallucinosis with maladaptive behavioral changes, characteristic perceptual changes, anxiety, depression, ideas of reference, fears of losing one's mind, paranoid ideation, impaired judgment, or impaired social or occupational functioning (Table 10). There may be intensification of

TABLE 10. **DSM-III-R Diagnostic Criteria for Hallucinogen Hallucinosis**

A. Recent use of a hallucinogen.

B. Maladaptive behavioral changes, e.g., marked anxiety or depression, ideas of reference, fear of losing one's mind, paranoid ideation, impaired judgment, impaired social or occupational functioning.

C. Perceptual changes occurring in a state of full wakefulness and alertness, e.g., subjective intensification of perceptions, depersonalization, derealization, illusions, hallucinations, synesthesias.

D. At least two of the following signs:
   (1) pupillary dilation
   (2) tachycardia
   (3) sweating
   (4) palpitations
   (5) blurring of vision
   (6) tremors
   (7) incoordination

E. Not due to any physical or other mental disorder.

*Note.* Reprinted with permission from the *Diagnostic and Statistical Manual of Mental Disorders.* Third Edition, Revised. Copyright © 1987 American Psychiatric Association.

perceptions, depersonalization, derealization, illusions, hallucinations, and seeing colors where a sound occurs. There may be hyperacusis and overattention to detail. Illusions may involve distortions of body image. Hallucinations are generally visual; more rarely, there may be auditory and tactile hallucinations. Physical symptoms include pupillary dilation, tachycardia, sweating, palpitations, blurring of vision, tremors, and incoordination. Euphoria and sense of mystical or religious experience may be accompanied by a sense of achieving insights not otherwise obtainable. The hallucinosis usually lasts eight to 12 hours. With LSD and some other hallucinogens, it may last one to three days.

## HALLUCINOGEN DELUSIONAL DISORDER AND MOOD DISORDERS

Hallucinogen delusional disorder may be brief or lead into a long-lasting psychotic episode that is difficult to distinguish from schizophreniform disorder. A delusional conviction exists that the disturbed perceptions and thoughts of hallucinogen hallucinosis correspond to reality. Hallucinogen mood disorder may also occur after hallucinogen use with appearance of depression and anxiety, and rarely with elation.

## POSTHALLUCINOGEN PERCEPTION DISORDER

Posthallucinogen perception disorder ("flashbacks") following cessation of hallucinogen use is marked by reexperiencing of one or more of the same perceptual symptoms that were experienced while intoxicated with the hallucinogen. It usually is fleeting but rarely may be more lasting and persistent. The diagnosis is made when these symptoms cause severe distress. It may be marked by noticing of trails, intensified flashes of colors, auditory visual hallucinations, and false perceptions of movement. Symptoms may be triggered by drug use or emergence into a dark environment and may be brought on by intention.

## ■ CANNABIS

Substances most commonly used in this class include marijuana, hashish, and purified delta-9-tetrahydrocannabinol

(THC). Most often smoked, these substances may also be mixed with food and eaten. Purity of marijuana varies and has generally increased from 1 to 5 percent in the 1960s to 10 to 15 percent in the 1980s. Dependence is marked by daily, or almost daily, use of cannabis. Abuse is characterized by episodic use with maladaptive behavior, such as driving while impaired. The definitions of abuse and dependence follow those of other disorders as in Table 5 and 6, without a characteristic withdrawal syndrome.

## CANNABIS INTOXICATION AND CANNABIS DELUSIONAL DISORDER

Intoxication after smoking cannabis reaches a peak after 10 to 30 minutes and lasts approximately three hours; metabolites may have a half-life of approximately 50 hours. The psychoactive effects of the drug are determined in major ways by the interaction of drug, person, and setting. Automobile accidents may result from cannabis intoxication, associated with impaired motor coordination. First-time users may not experience altered consciousness. Cannabis intoxication effects include euphoria, anxiety, suspiciousness or paranoid ideation, sensation of slowed time, impaired judgment, and social withdrawal. Inappropriate laughter, panic attacks, and dysphoric affects may also occur. Adverse reactions may be more common in patients with psychiatric disorders and in those who are frightened about the drug-taking situation. At least two of the following signs develop within two hours of cannabis use: 1) conjunctival infection, 2) increased appetite, 3) dry mouth, and 4) tachycardia. Toxicology is used to confirm the diagnosis.

Cannabis delusional disorder is an organic delusional syndrome usually with persecutory delusions that develop shortly after cannabis use. It may be associated with marked anxiety, emotional lability, and depersonalization, and may be misdiagnosed as schizophrenia. Subsequent amnesia for the episode can also occur.

## ■ NICOTINE

Disorders associated with smoking tobacco have been included with other substance use disorders, starting with DSM-III and continuing in DSM-III-R. The addictive constituent in tobacco is nicotine, which has euphoric effects and reinforcement properties similar to cocaine and opioids. Phenomena of tolerance and withdrawal occur with craving, irritability, anxiety, difficulty concentrating, and restlessness. As part of the withdrawal, there is also decreased heart rate, increased eating, increased sleep disturbance, and decreased alcohol intake. A variety of forms of nicotine dependence exists (i.e., cigarettes, pipe, cigars, snuff, and chewing tobacco). Dependence on nicotine frequently is continued even in those who have serious physical symptoms that are aggravated by smoking. Cigarette smoking generally has a familial pattern and may have a modest genetic contribution.

## ■ INHALANTS

Inhalants such as aliphatic and aromatic hydrocarbons found in gasoline, glue, paint thinners, and spray paints as well as halogenated hydrocarbons found in cleaners, typewriter correction fluid, and spray-can propellants and other volatile compounds containing esters, ketones, and glycols are included in this classification. These drugs may be used interchangeably. Use may depend on availability and experience. It is usually difficult to determine the exact substance responsible for the disorder. Other substances such as anesthetic gases and short-acting vasodilators such as amyl and butyl nitrites are classified as psychoactive substance dependence not otherwise specified and are listed separately. Rags soaked with the abused substance tend to be applied to the mouth and nose and the vapors breathed in, or they may be placed in a paper or plastic bag and the gases in the bag inhaled.

The effects of inhalant intoxication include belligerence, assaultiveness, apathy, impaired judgment, and impaired social or occupational functioning. Signs include dizziness, nystagmus, incoordination, slurred speech, unsteady gait, lethargy, depressed reflexes, psychomotor retardation, tremor, generalized muscle weakness, blurred vision or diplopia, stupor or coma, and euphoria. Diagnosis is confirmed by toxicology.

## ■ CAFFEINE

Caffeine, in the form of coffee, tea, cola, chocolate, and cocoa, is widely used. Caffeine is also present in over-the-counter analgesics, cold preparations, and stimulants. Caffeine-withdrawal headaches may occur, but they are usually not severe enough to require treatment. Caffeine intoxication can lead to restlessness, nervousness, excitement, insomnia, flushed face, diuresis, and gastrointestinal complaints. Doses leading to intoxication can vary. At high doses, there can be psychotic phenomena, cardiac arrhythmias, and psychomotor agitation. Mild sensory disturbances can occur at higher doses; at enormous doses, grand mal seizures and respiratory failure may result in death.

## ■ POLYSUBSTANCE DEPENDENCE

This category is used when in the period of the last six months, the individual has repeatedly used at least three categories of psychoactive substances (not including nicotine and caffeine) and no single psychoactive substance has predominated. Criteria for dependence has been met as a group, but not for any specific substance.

Primary versus secondary drugs of abuse have been categorized by chronology, preference, severity of abuse, and presence or absence of dependence. For example, a primary cocaine dependence may manifest with secondary alcohol abuse. In an attempt to self-medicate the dysphoria, restlessness, anxiety, and insomnia of cocaine intoxication, alcohol intake may result in secondary dependence. Patients will frequently tend to minimize the extent of these secondary drugs. Without a thorough substance use history, a diagnosed primary cocaine abuser may unexpectedly develop alcohol withdrawal symptoms.

### EPIDEMIOLOGY

Estimates of polysubstance dependence in outpatient alcohol clinics are greater than 50 percent. As alcohol dependence is becoming more of a "young man's disease" (the median age for the typical alcohol abuser is between age 20 and 30), there is an increasing overlap with the age group typical for drug abuse. Marijuana and cigarette abuse typically start in adolescence, heroin abuse in the 18- to 24-age bracket, and cocaine abuse in the adolescent and young adult range. In methadone maintenance programs, 40 to 70 percent of patients are alcoholics. These patients may develop new-onset alcoholism or manifest an exacerbation of a long-standing problem.

## COMBINATIONS

Often one drug is used in combination to counterbalance the side effects or to potentiate the effect of another drug. Heroin and cocaine are used iv as a combination called "speed balling." This combination is said to mute the dysphoric side effects of cocaine. Speed balling can be particularly lethal. Another highly lethal combination is glutethimide (Doriden) and cocaine. This combination has produced an epidemic of overdose cases in certain urban areas, especially among teenagers, and potentiates central nervous system (CNS) respiratory depression. Pentazocine (Talwin) and diphenhydramine (Benadryl), street-named "T's and Blues," combines two prescription medications that produce intoxication. Virtually any combination of alcohol and other drugs is seen. Marijuana is often so pervasive in this population that it is not perceived as a drug of abuse.

## CHOICE OF DRUG

Theories of addiction have attempted to develop psychological profiles of drug abusers and explain choice of drug. For example, heroin may be used to ward off aggressive impulses. Some polysubstance abusers may use substances indiscriminately rather than seeking the specific pharmacologic properties of any one drug. This may be due to basic needs for relief of pain, avoidance of reality, or a need to change and control aspects of consciousness. Choice of drugs of abuse may also depend on such factors as availability, peer influence, and economics. Polysubstance abusers tend to be younger and in greater denial of a treatment goal of total abstinence and present without medical complications to any particular drug.

## *ADDICTION SUBSTITUTION*

Frequently, there is resistance to the treatment concept of total abstinence, and one drug may be abused in place of another. Education is needed to make patients aware of the relapse potential of abusing a substance that is associated and conditioned to the primary drug of choice.

In addition, the medical hazards of heavy tobacco use in a recovering population have been inadequately dealt with in most treatment programs.

## ■ DIAGNOSTIC DILEMMAS

The diagnostic dilemma presented by the substance abusing patient challenges the clinician with medical, neurologic, and psychiatric disturbances that need careful systematic evaluation. It is hard to determine whether and when to treat intoxication, withdrawal, and chronic effects, and complications or additional Axis I disorder; and whether Axis II characteristics are state- or trait-related. Complications such as acquired immune deficiency syndrome (AIDS) dementia and exacerbation of underlying personality characteristics have important implications for management and disposition. This difficulty with differential diagnoses should instill some degree of humility and conservatism.

Often the underlying pathology is not readily identified. Conservative management with a careful review of the medical, psychiatric, and substance abuse histories; physical and mental status examinations; laboratory tests; and third-party information can clarify the diagnoses. In other cases, only time and observation clarifies etiology.

## *SIGNS AND SYMPTOMS*

Alcoholic and substance abusing patients have frequent medical and neurologic complications that alter mental status. AIDS dementia, seizure phenomenon, head trauma, and serious infections may alter mental status. Closely following signs and symptoms helps in the differential diagnosis. Rapid pulse and elevated temperature may indicate infection, withdrawal, or drug toxicity. Abnormal pulse may indicate intoxication with sympathomimetic drugs (e.g., cocaine or amphetamine), withdrawal from CNS depressants (e.g., alcohol or benzodiazepines), or cardiac arryhthmia from overdose. A slow heart rate could indicate opiate intoxication, severe head trauma, or cardiac conduction delays. Abnormal pupil size or oculogyric movements can help clarify various drug overdose situations. Constricted pinpoint pupils in a comatose patient may signal the possibility of opioid overdose. Dilated pupils are associated with sympathomimetic intoxication. Gaze palsies, confusion, and ataxia could be secondary to thiamine deficiency leading to Wernicke's encephalopathy. Nystagmus and agitation could lead to the diagnosis of PCP intoxication.

In approaching a differential between overdose, withdrawal, chronic organicity, or psychiatric diagnoses, it is most important to rule out or treat life-threatening conditions first. If taken in high enough dosages, most substances (e.g., opioids, CNS depressants, cocaine, PCP) can result in overdose mortality. For a patient with an unexplained coma, standard life support protocols should be employed. A brief but thorough physical examination can detect fresh needle marks, recent alcohol intake, or nasal irritation from cocaine or inhalant abuse. History from those acquainted with the patient is useful. Intubation and gastric lavage with depressant-induced coma; use of naloxone for opioid overdose; and prompt treatment of seizures, acidosis, and elevated temperature with cocaine toxicity can be life saving. In differentiating withdrawal from other toxic psychosis, there is more autonomic hyperactivity, more disorientation, a less fixed delusional system, and more memory loss following the psychosis.

Markedly altered mental status, evidence of recent substance abuse intake, and reliable corroborating history can help in distinguishing between withdrawal, chronic organicity, or functional diagnoses. In patients with a known chronic substance abuse history, unreliable recent history, and prior history of major psychiatric symptoms, diagnoses may be delayed or provisional. For example, an intoxicated paranoid patient with a known history of paranoid schizophrenia and polysubstance abuse could present with a differential diagnosis including simple intoxication, alcohol hallucinosis, delirium tremens, drug intoxication, meningitis or space-occupying lesion, postconcussive syndrome, seizure phenomena, neuroleptic malignant syndrome, or rare apparent delirium secondary to an exacerbation of a functional psychiatric illness. Long-standing organicity can confuse the diagnostic picture when it is not previously known. Alcohol dementia and postconcussive head syndromes can sensitize the brain to react to minor substance abuse with dramatic and unpredictable results. In such patients, many things are going on at the same time. It is important to provide a safe environment; to protect the patient and others from harm, and to ensure basic airway, respiratory, and cardiac support until a basic diagnostic workup is completed.

## DIFFICULT-TO-MANAGE PATIENTS

Dual diagnosis patients with major characterological difficulties secondary to antisocial, paranoid, histrionic, or borderline features may present with an exacerbation of primitive defenses (e.g., projection, projective identification, and splitting during intoxication). Often these patients may become belligerent, distrustful, unappreciative, uncooperative, or violent, making management and history taking difficult. Due to the strong countertransference feelings these patients evoke, inappropriate treatment decisions may ensue. Before making a very unusual treatment decision or participating in uncharacteristic behavior with a patient, consultation with another expert may be helpful. Sometimes a simple "time-out" for the therapist to collect thoughts and feelings may be helpful. These feelings should not be ignored, but used to help clarify diagnostic possibilities. Frequently, obnoxious, uncooperative, destructive behavior or apparent personality problems are time limited and related to intoxication, withdrawal, or organic states. They may reflect the patient's fear and low self-esteem. A totally uncooperative patient, if tolerated through the acute intoxication, can have a dramatic and unexpected turnaround.

## WITHDRAWAL SYNDROMES

Major withdrawal syndromes occur with CNS depressants and opiates; they are less pronounced with sympathomimetics (e.g., cocaine, amphetamines). Alcohol withdrawal syndrome should be suspected with recent cessation of intake (12 to 48 hours) or substantial lowering of BAL. Elevated pulse, blood pressure, and temperature; mild tremor; and nausea or vomiting are associated symptoms. Benzodiazepine withdrawal may be heralded by seizures seven to eight days after last ingestion. Opioid flu-like withdrawal symptoms subjectively may be quite disturbing to patients, although they are rarely life threatening. Cocaine withdrawal may be punctuated by severe depression and suicidal ideation. It is important to identify and treat withdrawal symptoms early to avoid complications.

## ■ INTERACTION WITH OTHER PSYCHIATRIC DISORDERS

In recent years, greater clarity has been brought to bear in terms of the reliability and the validity of psychiatric diagnosis. This development has helped researchers in the substance abuse field to evaluate the complex interactions that exist between substance abuse and other psychiatric disorders. "Dual diagnosis patients," patients who have a substance abuse disorder in addition to another major psychiatric diagnosis, have strained the mental health treatment system. Important work needs to be done to understand further the epidemiology of these interactions, causal associations, and natural histories. Multidisciplinary treatment strategies have yet to be perfected to treat these difficult, often recalcitrant patients.

The interaction of psychiatric disorders may be manifold. Major psychiatric disorders may precede the development of substance abuse, develop concurrently, or manifest secondarily. Psychiatric disorders may precipitate the onset or modify the course of a substance abuse disorder. Psychiatric disorders and substance abuse may present as independent conditions. In practical clinical terms, this "chicken and egg" dilemma makes it difficult at any one cross-section of time to differentiate symptoms of withdrawal, intoxication, and secondary cognitive, affective, perceptual, or personality changes from underlying psychiatric disorders. Important tools in differential diagnosis include careful history taking, urine screens, and determining the course or sequence of symptoms. Critical information is obtained from third parties. Family history of psychiatric illness (including substance abuse) can, in some cases, help the diagnosis. Recent research has aimed at developing reliable trait markers for psychiatric and substance abuse disorders.

Early theorists described a broad-based vulnerability to mental illness taking the form of psychiatric disorders or substance abuse based on factors such as sex, family upbringing, environment, or personal history. More recent studies have questioned these approaches. Utilizing sophisticated family research techniques, these studies have shown that the severity of abuse has not predicted greater general psychopathology in family members and that several disorders that clinically present together (e.g., affective disorders, antisocial personality, and alcoholism) have separate genetic transmission.

McLellan, Woody, and O'Brien at the University of Pennsylvania developed research instruments to study severity of illness in several areas. One major conclusion of this research was that severity of psychiatric illness, regardless of specific diagnosis, is negatively related to treatment outcome. Individuals with high psychiatric severity ratings have poor outcomes. Differential therapeutics and matching patients to programs resulted from this basic research and will be discussed in Chapter 8.

One fairly consistent finding across addictive disorders is that chronic intoxication eventually leads to dysphoric mood states. Regardless of the patient's expectation, or experiences of euphoria during chronic use, chronic psychiatric symptoms (e.g., major depressive symptoms) occur late in the course of addictive disorder. This may be the result of altered neurotransmitters or neuroreceptors, hormonal or metabolic changes, chronic demoralization, grief from personal losses, or result from stresses of the addictive life-style. Chronic heroin use has the tendency to lead to lethargy and social withdrawal. Sustained alcohol ingestion generally produces depression and anxiety, even though brief periods of euphoria may be still be evident.

## AFFECTIVE DISORDERS

Prevalence of affective disorders in substance abuse patients depends largely on what instruments are used and at what cross-section of time symptoms are measured. Several reviews are available, highlighting the wide range of instruments used to study depression in alcoholics (4). Clinical interviews show lower rates of depression of approximately 33 percent compared to instruments with rates of up to 70 percent. Schuckit estimated that between one-quarter to two-thirds of alcoholics will have severe depressive symptoms at some point in their alcoholic careers (5). However, only 5 to 10 percent of alcoholics have an independent affective disorder. Schuckit cited five factors that produce this clinical picture: 1) alcohol can cause depressive symptoms in anyone, presumably by its toxic effect on the brain; 2) signs of temporary depression can follow prolonged drinking; 3) drinking can escalate during a primary affective disorder; 4) depression and alcohol problems occur along with other psychiatric disorders, especially antisocial personality disorder; and 5) only a small portion of patients have independent alcoholism and affective disorders. In less than 10 percent of depressed patients is alcoholism a secondary problem.

While the majority of alcoholics will not have an independent diagnosis of major depressive disorder, other less severe depressive disorders may persist in a large proportion of alcoholics after cessation of drinking. Other causes of depression in alcoholics could include other substance abuse, trauma, or social losses. Drinking may be more of a problem during a hypomanic or manic phase of a bipolar disorder than the depressed phase. In the majority of cases, depressive symptomatology subsides after three to four weeks of abstinence and usually needs no pharmacologic intervention. Use of antidepressants is indicated after a drug-free period, and abstinence is required for efficacy. Lithium is indicated when bipolar affective illness is present. Alprazolam should be avoided because of addictive potential in this population. There is evidence that untreated major depression in a primary alcoholic or secondary alcoholism in a primary depressive patient may worsen prognosis.

## DEPRESSION AND OPIATES

There is considerable evidence that depression is higher in active opioid users and may subside with abstinence (6). Major depression ranges from 17 to 28 percent in heroin addicts and is considerably higher among methadone clients. Affective disorders in general have ranged as high as 60 percent. Many depressive episodes are mild, may be related to treatment seeking, and are related to stress. Depression has been found to be a poor prognostic sign on two-and-a-half-year follow-up, except in cases of coexistent, antisocial personality, in which depression improves prognosis.

## DEPRESSION AND COCAINE

Affective disorders have been reported concurrently in 30 percent of cocaine addicts, with a significant proportion of these patients being bipolar or cylothymic (7). Bipolar manic patients may use cocaine to heighten feelings of grandiosity. The profound dysphoric mood related to cocaine binges will resolve in the majority of cocaine addicts. A minority of patients may have underlying unipolar or bipolar disorder, which needs to be treated separately. This abstinence dysphoria may be secondary to depletion of brain catecholamines (e.g., dopamine) or to alteration in neural receptors, with resultant postsynaptic supersensitivity.

## SUBSTANCE ABUSE AND PSYCHOSIS

Psychotic symptomatology can result from the use of a wide range of psychoactive substances: alcohol, cocaine, phencyclidine, hallucinogens, and inhalants. All have organic syndromes that mimic various functional psychiatric syndromes. Opioids, however, have shown some antipsychotic properties.

More complex is the relationship between schizophrenia and substance abuse. Various studies have shown a propensity for schizophrenics to abuse substances (8). The role of substance abuse in precipitating or altering the course of an underlying schizophrenic disorder is unclear. Substance abuse may exacerbate symptoms in well-controlled schizophrenics. Alcohol, marijuana, or cocaine abuse may produce psychotic symptoms that persist only in vulnerable individuals. It may be that schizophrenics seek out certain types of drugs for self-medication. Schizophrenics also use tobacco and caffeine more often than controlled populations. Tobacco use has been associated with lowering of blood levels of neuroleptics and a requirement of higher-than-average doses of neuroleptics for symptom control. Schizophrenic patients may seek out drugs that increase the chance of precipitating psychotic episodes to feel a sense of mastery or to experience merging. Schizophrenic patients may be treating dysphoria, or negative symptoms of their disease, and use stimulants to allow them to feel more intensely. These patients may also be treating extrapyramidal or sedative side effects of neuroleptic medications. Schizophrenic patients who abuse stimulant drugs may also be treating an independent, underlying affective disorder. Substance abuse may provide the schizophrenic patient with the experience of control over unpredictable states of consciousness or may provide a strong identity as a substance abuser, which may be more palatable and perceived as being less stigmatic than having a major psychiatric disorder. Phenothiazines may be indicated, and compliance with properly taking medications may be more of a problem in this group.

## ANXIETY DISORDERS

Generalized anxiety disorder, posttraumatic stress disorder, panic disorder, and phobic disorder are overrepresented in substance abuse patients, especially alcoholics and sedative-hypnotic abusers. One study of alcoholics reported general anxiety disorder in 9 percent, and phobias in 3 percent, significantly higher than the general population (9). Posttraumatic stress syndrome has been related to the high rates of alcoholism in Vietnam veterans who saw active duty. Panic disorder has been found in 5 percent of inpatient addicts.

High dosages of benzodiazepines up to 1,000 or 1,500 mg have been reported in patients with underlying anxiety disorders. These patients are often very difficult to treat due to the complex interaction between the anxiety and the substance abuse disorder. In treatment of addicted patients with anxiety disorders, benzodiazepines should be avoided if possible. Specific treatment of the underlying anxiety disorder may include antidepressants, monoamine oxidase inhibitors, buspirone, or propranolol.

## NEUROPSYCHIATRIC IMPAIRMENT

Chronic abuse of alcohol, sedatives, and inhalants have been well correlated with chronic, irreversible brain damage and neuropsychological impairment. These impairments may be gross, as evidenced in alcohol dementia or Korsakoff's syndrome, or relatively mild and detected only by neuropsychological testing.

Cognitive impairment may be short-lived and recede after three to four weeks of abstinence, improve gradually over several months or years of abstinence, or be permanent. Alcohol's damage to brain tissue has been chronicled by abnormal computed tomography (CT)-scan findings (cortical atrophy), altered EEG (decreased alpha activity), and altered evoked potential (decreased P3 component). Brain damage may be secondary to an as-yet-unknown interaction between the direct toxic effect on the brain, liver damage, hormonal changes, and trauma. Chronic alcohol use causes significant impairment in new learning, short-term memory, concept formation, problem solving, and judgment. Similar cognitive deficits have been found with chronic benzodiazepine and inhalant abuse.

Tarter and Edwards have retrospectively demonstrated in histories of alcoholics an increased incidence of childhood hyperactivity (10). These alcoholics have best resembled the early onset, familial, or primary alcoholics and alcoholics who have early onsets of problem drinking, social incompetency, and maladjustment.

# ■ REFERENCES

1. American Psychiatric Association: Diagnostic and Statistical Manual of Mental Disorders, 3rd ed. Washington, DC, American Psychiatric Association, 1980
2. American Psychiatric Association: Diagnostic and Statistical Manual of Mental Disorders, 3rd ed, revised. Washington, DC, American Psychiatric Association, 1987
3. Frances RJ, Franklin JE: Alcohol and other psychoactive substance use disorders, in Textbook of Psychiatry. Edited by Hales R, Talbott J. Washington, DC, American Psychiatric Press, 1988
4. Frances RJ, Franklin J: Primary prevention of alcoholism and substance abuse, in Primary Prevention in Psychiatry: State of the Art. Edited by Talbott S, Barter J. Washington, DC, American Psychiatric Press, 1986
5. Schuckit MA: Genetic and clinical implications of alcoholism and affective disorder. Am J Psychiatry 1986; 43:140–147
6. Khantzian EJ, Treece C: DSM-III psychiatric diagnosis of narcotic addicts: recent findings. Arch Gen Psychiatry 1985; 42:1067–1071

7. Weiss RD, Mirin SM: Subtypes of cocaine abusers. Psychiatr Clin North Am 1986; 9:491–501
8. Schneier FR, Siris SG: A review of psychoactive substance use and abuse in schizophrenia: patterns of drug choice. J Nerv Ment Dis 1987; 175:641
9. Ross HE, Glaser FB, Germanson T: The prevalence of psychiatric disorders in patients with alcohol and other drug problems. Arch Gen Psychiatry 1988; 45:1023–1031
10. Tarter RE, Edwards K: Psychological factors associated with the risk for alcoholism. Alcoholism: Clinical and Experimental Research 1988; 12:471–479

# SUBSTANCE ABUSE DISORDERS IN THE GENERAL HOSPITAL AND IN THE WORKPLACE

**5**

## ■ THE GENERAL HOSPITAL

It has been estimated that 25 to 50 percent of general hospital admissions are related to complications of psychoactive substance abuse (1). A high index of suspicion may help the health care provider to detect a hidden addictive disorder. There may be further advantages in confronting the addictive process during a medical crisis when denial may be lessened or can be easily confronted by irrefutable medical evidence. Alcoholism may be diagnosed by associated medical problems, such as liver disease, pancreatitis, anemia, certain types of pneumonia, delirium, dementia, gastric ulcers, esophageal varices, tuberculosis, or symptoms mimicking psychiatric syndromes.

## ADMISSION WORKUP

Detailed alcohol and substance histories should be taken on admission for every patient in the general hospital setting. Information should be gathered in a straightforward manner in concert with the rest of the medical history. When problems do exist, answers may be vague, evasive, or aggressively defensive. In early abuse patterns, some patients may be surprised by the connection between their substance use and their current medical problems. Health professionals should be knowledgeable of the components of a basic alcohol and substance history (Table 11). Due to denial, resistance, organicity, and psychiatric symptoms, a consultation with an addiction specialist may be helpful in making a diagnosis. Third-party sources such as family or friends may be necessary to obtain crucial information. For example, addi-

TABLE 11.  **Components of a Basic Alcohol and Substance Use History**

- Chief complaint

- History of present illness

- Current medical signs and symptoms

- Substance abuse review of symptoms (ROS) for all psychoactive substances

- Dates of first use, regular use, heaviest use, longest period of sobriety, pattern, amount, frequency, time of last use, route of administration, circumstances of use, reactions to use

- Medical history, medications, HIV status

- History of past substance abuse treatment, response to treatment

- Family history, including substance abuse history

- Psychiatric history

- Legal history

- Object relations history

- Personal history

tional corroboration is needed in the assessment of prior alcohol abuse in a man who was admitted two days earlier for routine surgery, denied alcohol abuse on admission, but appears to be in early delirium tremens. The psychoactive substance abuse history should be a systematic review of all the major drug classes. Often patients will not consider a particular substance a "drug." For example, a 30-year-old woman who had been smoking marijuana every day since college did not associate marijuana as a drug. Asking "Do you abuse drugs?" seemed to her a pejorative question. She did not offer the desired information due to a lack of knowledge and a particular view of the stigma of drug abuse.

## SPECIFIC SUBSTANCE HISTORY TAKING

Experience with drug classes such as alcohol, opioids, cocaine or other stimulants, tranquilizers, hallucinogens, marijuana, inhalants, and over-the-counter medication should be systematically ascertained. Use and possible abuse of prescription medications should be covered. The history should include the type of liquor or specific drug, amount, pattern or frequency of use, and time of last use. The later historical information may be very important in distinguishing various organic mental states. The route of administration, oral or iv or pulmonary inhalation, may have important health consequences. For example, HIV screening should be done on the vast majority of iv drug addicts presenting for admission in the general hospital setting. If alcohol abuse is suspected, symptoms of physical dependence must be actively pursued. Missing such information can be life threatening.

A history of early morning tremors or shakes, a subjective need for a drink to calm the nerves, elevated pulse and blood pressure, or a known past history of alcoholism seizures or delirium tremens should signal the need for pharmacologic detoxification. Polysubstance abuse may mask underlying physical dependence on one prominent psychoactive substance (e.g., opioids in "speed balling" or "hits," alcohol dependence secondary to cocaine addiction). Past history of hospitalization for motor vehicle accidents, accidental injuries, or substance-related violence should be sought in addition to any history of treatment for alcohol or other substance abuse problems.

## PSYCHIATRIC CONSULTATION
## TO GENERAL FLOORS

Consultations from general hospital floors may be straight-forward requests for substance abuse evaluation or more cryptic requests for evaluation of organicity, mood disorders, or acting-out behavior. Often these patients are perceived by house staff as being manipulative, demanding, and unappreciative. Often in reality, they can present as such. It is important not to disavow the staff's real feelings but provide a framework of understanding of the addictive process that can make these feelings meaningful and tolerable. Self-awareness of feelings induced by patients is not only diagnostic at times, but also may relieve the guilt of retaliatory fantasies. Few people go into medicine to dislike their patients. Having these feelings surface may be intolerable to some house staff. In affective illnesses, the presence of over-whelming affects may focus attention away from a concomitant addictive process. In cases of organicity, important historical information may simply be forgotten.

Each consultation request should be reviewed in an attempt to ascertain most clearly what is being requested. Frequently, this requires a call to the referring physician. Questions of confidentiality may come up with patients regarding their substance abuse. Generally, confidentiality needs to be discussed and handled appropriately. Because honesty is one of the core treatment tools in an addictive disease process, conspiracies or secrets regarding substance abuse are not advisable.

## ASSESSING THE CHART

As a consultant, reviewing the medical chart in detail is essential, not only to pick up important information about admitting signs and symptoms, third-party statements, and mental status, but also to put together divergent clues of substance abuse in a fresh manner. Pertinent laboratory work, X rays, EEG, computed tomography (CT) scans, and so on should be reviewed. Suggestions for additional laboratory work (e.g., magnesium levels in a patient with a history of delirium tremens) should be made.

## THE INTERVIEW

If the consult request asks for assessment of a substance abuse problem, this should be clearly stated to the patient early in the interview. The referring physician can be asked to join the interview if it seems appropriate. In writing up findings, it is best briefly to view impressions of the reason for the consultation, identifying information, a brief history of present illness, past history, medical complications, medications, and mental status. The impressions and recommendations should be prominent and the focus of the consult. Often this message is the only one read.

## TREATMENT PLANNING

Specific recommendations for treatment range from outpatient substance abuse treatment to no further intervention, to inpatient substance abuse or psychiatric treatment. Often active treatment must be postponed until the acute medical problems are stabilized. For patients showing early abuse patterns, simple counseling, education, and appropriate reassurance may be all that is necessary. If the patient does not have marked medical or psychiatric complications, is motivated, has a less serious abuse pattern and little prior treatment exposure, outpatient referral is preferable. Inpatient psychiatric treatment may be indicated when major psychiatric illnesses need to be treated (psychosis, major depression) or with suicidal or homicidal ideation. Many units for mentally ill chemically abusing patients have been created to treat the substance abuser with major psychiatric problems (2). Transfer to an inpatient rehabilitation unit, when indicated, should be direct transfer from the hospital to the treatment facility. All detoxification regimens should be clearly and explicitly spelled out. It may be necessary to work with the treatment staff to modify regimens in case of medical complications, such as liver or renal disease.

## ADDITIONAL TREATMENT ISSUES

It is important to realize that abstinence in itself is not evidence of satisfactory treatment; a patient can be free of drug or alcohol use or craving while in the hospital and quickly return to active use on discharge. Family and individual education about substance abuse and assessment of the meaning of drugs or alcohol use in that person's life can begin in the hospital. Drug urine screens or alcohol breathalyzer tests may need to be obtained on general hospital inpatients. Occasionally, patients will find methods to use substances even while in the hospital. These patients should be in closed units, where articles and people entering can be monitored for contraband. Early confrontation of continuing alcohol or drug use may clear up complicated diagnostic pictures.

## MAKING THE REFERRAL

It is often best that the patient make the initial call. It is also important that all calls be made while in the hospital setting and appointments set before discharge. In cases where substance abuse treatment facilities are connected with the general hospital, in-house contact is advised, as is attendance at in-house meetings, such as Alcoholics Anonymous (AA), when feasible.

## DRUG INTERACTION

Special attention to drug interactions should be made in the general hospital setting. When first admitted, patients may have psychoactive drugs in their system that will adversely interact with prescribed medications. Table 12 outlines the effects of prescribed medication interactions with alcohol.

## MANAGEMENT OF PAIN

A major concern of staff in treating substance abuse patients in the general hospital setting is iatrogenic contributions to addiction. This is most notable in iv drug addicts for whom pain medication is required. Many staff members are schooled to be very cautious and suspicious when prescribing pain medication with these patients. Excessive caution can lead to undermedication. These patients may present with low frustration tolerance, anxiety, demandingness, and manipulation. It must be stressed, however, that these patients do experience pain, and if too much rage and anger is evoked in the staff, this may drive treatment personnel unconsciously to punish offensive patients by undermedicating them. In certain individuals, even larger doses of pain medications are indicated due to tolerance. Each patient should

TABLE 12. **Effects of Prescribed Medication Interactions with Alcohol**

| | |
|---|---|
| Disulfiram (Antabuse) | Flushing, diaphoresis, vomiting, confusion |
| Anticoagulants (oral) | Increased effect with acute intoxication, decreased effect after chronic use |
| Antimicrobials | Minor Antabuse reactions |
| Tranquilizers, narcotics, antihistamines | Increased central nervous system depression |
| Diazepam | Increased absorption |
| Phenytoin | Increased anticonvulsant effect with acute intoxication; alcohol intoxication or withdrawal may lower seizure threshold after chronic alcohol abuse |
| Salicylates | Gastrointestinal bleeding |
| Chlorpromazine | Increased levels of alcohol |
| Monoamine oxidase inhibitors | Adverse reactions to tyramine in some alcoholic beverages |

*Note.* Reprinted with permission from Frances RJ, Franklin JE Jr: Alcohol and Other Psychoactive Substance Use Disorders, in *The American Psychiatric Press Textbook of Psychiatry.* Edited by Talbott JA, Hales RE, Yudofsky, SC. Washington, DC, American Psychiatric Press, 1988. Copyright © 1988 American Psychiatric Press.

be evaluated carefully, looking at past history, pattern of abuse, personality, and physical pathology. When substance abuse patients' concerns and requests are categorically dismissed, serious prejudicial attitudes may be evident. In some cases, staff should remove themselves from the patient's care before a spiral develops that will end up in the abandonment of the patient.

Chronic pain patients have a high profile for abusing drugs. The concept of "pain behavior" has been recognized. The "Madison" is an acronym for scoring this behavior and includes assessment of such factors as variable pain patterns, strong needs to authenticate the pain, denial of emotional problems, pain associated with interpersonal relationships, feelings of being unique, idealization then devaluation of doctors, and the feeling that nothing helps. Maintaining continuity of care and promoting realistic expectations are prominent treatment goals. It is necessary to avoid intramuscular (im) medication and prn dose scheduling and to ensure adequate coverage (i.e., selection of medications that have adequate half-lives for dosage scheduling, appropriate administration, and the right medication for type of pain) (3).

**ORGAN TRANSPLANTS**

Increasing numbers of organ transplants will be performed in the next few years. Mental health personnel will be asked to assess patients' psychological readiness to receive such transplants. In developing criteria for eligibility for heart or liver transplants, alcoholism will need to be considered a complicating factor. Active alcoholism has been a contraindication for liver transplantation, although controversy surrounds this issue. The question of evaluating recovering alcoholics is a complicated issue. It has been estimated that 30 percent of liver cirrhosis is secondary to alcoholism. Care must be taken not to discriminate against a stable recovering alcoholic who may well be a good candidate for transplant. The fear of relapse, which would undermine the benefits of this treatment, is a consideration; however, careful evaluation and certain criteria may diminish this risk. Such criteria might include at least two years of sobriety from alcohol, no other active substance abuse, and good family support. The recovering alcoholic may be able to be evaluated in line with other candidates.

# ■ THE WORKPLACE

Increasingly in the past two decades, the military, a large number of major corporations, and insurance carriers have recognized the value of early identification and evaluation of chemical dependency problems and have offered their chemically dependent employees opportunities for treatment and assistance (4). Approximately 10,000 employee assistance programs (EAPs) help reduce costs associated with increased absenteeism and medical claims due to substance abuse. Many corporations have also established general fitness and wellness programs, which emphasize exercise, weight control, cessation of smoking, stress reduction, and detection of warning signs of illness. General Motors reported an 85 percent reduction in lost personnel; Kennecott Copper found a 50 percent decrease in absenteeism with EAPs (5). In addition to liability due to accidents, costly mistakes, and morale problems affecting co-workers of a troubled employee, considerable costs are incurred by firing, hiring, and retraining. The hidden benefits of rehabilitation programs are not lost on administrators concerned with cost effectiveness. In addition to retaining valuable employees, the corporations find that these programs reduce union pressure that could occur from firing employees whose job performances do not improve because they fail to follow through with treatment. Unions have recognized the valuable health benefits side of EAPs as a way of improving labor-management relations. Increasingly, unions are pressing to make the programs available to family members as part of benefit packages.

## CASE FINDING AT THE WORKPLACE

In our culture, the greatest pressure that leads substance abusers to accept treatment occurs in the workplace. Usually abusers do not seek help until a crisis has occurred somewhere in their lives. Frequently people will not seek treatment even through they may have marital, medical, or other problems until their jobs are threatened. Fellow employees and managers may be overprotective of a troubled employee and wait until a crisis occurs that leads to firing. It is helpful to train supervisors that early recognition of job performance problems and referral to an EAP for evaluation can result in protection of jobs as well as in improved health. Substance abusers who still have jobs and marriages intact have the best prognosis.

## THE EAP MODEL

Most EAPs have both voluntary and mandatory portals of entry. Once workers see the program is successful for others, many volunteer for treatment; the ratio of volunteer to compulsory referrals often exceeds 10 to 1. EAPs are most often run by the company with in-house counselors and are connected to personnel or medical departments. The employee can approach the

EAP representative voluntarily and confidentially before major job problems have arisen. Supervisors, union representatives, and employees are given educational materials on the warning signs of work performance problems and descriptions of the program. Supervisors document work-related problems and are encouraged not to make a diagnosis or speculate on the specific diagnosis of an employee's work problems. Supervisors suggest a meeting with the EAP counselor and, if the job is at stake, may make a mandatory referral to the EAP counselor. The employee who has had documented history of work-related problems may face a choice between acceptance of the referral or job action. This basically provides the employee with another opportunity to improve work performance with the addition of treatment. Information obtained during the process is not shared with the supervisor and is kept confidential. Ultimate job action depends on job performance rather than on the recommendation of either the EAP counselor or the treatment resource. Confidentiality is essential to any successful EAP. Companies have found that it is better to treat and retain recovering substance abusers than to have employees with undetected problems.

## JOB IMPAIRMENT

Employees may either have problems related to the use of substances on the job or the effects of chronic abuse that takes place after work hours. Disability may include medical, psychiatric, and social consequences of chronic use. Off-hours drinking and substance abuse can contribute to hangovers, withdrawal symptoms, absenteeism, medical and psychiatric complications, and preoccupation with obtaining or using the substances, which can interfere with concentration on the job. Off-duty problems such as charges of driving while intoxicated or drug possession charges are an embarrassment to a company, and legal and illegal off-hours substance abuse can affect employee morale. Use of substances can contribute to corruption and to white-collar crime. Military plane crashes have been found to be associated with use of marijuana, other substances, or alcohol either by ground crews or flyers. Impairment of physicians is a major problem for the profession. Companies tend to be more punitive for substance abuse than for alcohol. Many companies will require a "Ulysses" contract from substance abusers, which provides that the employees abstain from drugs and that the employer be notified and employment terminated if the employee returns to the habit. Better understanding of prevailing negative attitudes regarding the substance abuser and of the particular problems and needs of corporations that employ them will be important. The growing concern of corporate benefits departments requiring cost effectiveness is likely to lead to improvement and sharpening of measurable treatment goals.

## ■ REFERENCES

1. Crowley T, Chesluk D, Hart R: Drug and alcohol abuse among psychiatric admissions. Arch Gen Psychiatry 1974; 30:13–20
2. Frances RJ, Allen M: The interaction of substance-use disorders with nonpsychotic psychiatric disorders, in Psychiatry. Edited by Michels R. Philadelphia, JB Lippincott, 1986, pp 1–13
3. Hackett TP, Bouckoms A: The pain patient: evaluation and treatment, in Handbook of General Hospital Psychiatry, 2nd ed. Edited by Hackett TP, Cassem NH. Littleton, MA, PSG Publishing, 1988, pp 42–68
4. Frances RJ, Gold MS, Conroy A: Substance use disorders in the workplace, in Result of President's Advisors Conference, Caneel Bay PDLA. Edited by Gold M, Turner C. Princeton, NJ, PDLA, 1986, pp 38–42
5. Jones KR, Vischi TR: Impact of alcohol, drug abuse and mental health treatment on medical care utilization. Med Care 1979; 17 (suppl):1–82

# 6 LABORATORY FINDINGS AND DIAGNOSTIC INSTRUMENTS

■ **LABORATORY FINDINGS**

## *URINE AND BLOOD SCREEN*

In the absence of a clear history of psychoactive substance abuse, several physical signs and laboratory test results may be a tip-off of primary substance abuse disorder. There are several general findings that should heighten suspicion of drug abuse in unknown cases. Vital sign changes, agitation, irritability or unpredictable behavior, needle marks or scars, and evidence of unexplained trauma all may signal psychoactive substance abuse. Inadequate management of pain with unusual analgesic dosages and unexpected elevated blood levels (e.g., alcohol) without obvious intoxication may also signal drug or alcohol tolerance and addiction.

The use of urine and blood levels cannot be overstressed as a mechanism to screen for psychoactive substance abuse problems. The sensitivity and accuracy of blood and urine screening has improved with the addition of gas chromatography to more routine screening techniques. A general toxicology screen includes a blood alcohol level (BAL).

### SELECTION OF TOXICOLOGIC TESTS AND PHARMACOKINETICS

Knowledge of the half-life of various drug doses will help in making sense of results. For example, the half-life of 4 oz of orally administered ethyl alcohol will be one to two hours. A BAL of 200 mg/dl would indicate recent heavy intake and most likely current intoxication. A negative paper chromatography drug screen for cocaine in a man admitted for a two-day history of paranoid, delusional behavior will not rule out abuse because cocaine has a relatively short half-life (it clears in 24 to 36 hours) and because paper chromatography has a low sensitivity (1). Marijuana, which is highly fat soluble, has a relatively long half-life and can be detected in the urine in heavy users up to three weeks after last use.

Urine drug screen results usually are reported as either positive or negative for any particular drug. Most routine urine screens cover the major drugs of abuse. Specificity and sensitivity are lower with thin-layer chromatography and immunoassay techniques. More sophisticated and sensitive quantitative testing with gas chromatography-mass spectrometry (GCMS) can later be done with certain drugs (e.g., marijuana) if urine from the original sample is positive. Urine drug screens generally are not useful in court because they do not answer the question of degree of intoxication. Hair can also be analyzed to detect drug abuse. Blood samples are done in forensic cases. For general hospital purposes, urine drug screens are imperative in certain situations. In cases of unknown coma, in atypical psychiatric presentations, with agitated and confused patients, with known drug histories, or with physical evidence of substance abuse, urine drug screening should be routine. In high-risk populations or areas where drugs may be epidemic (e.g., certain inner-city general hospitals), urine drug screening should be routinely done for psychiatric admission.

## OTHER BLOOD SCREENING TESTS

Suspicion of alcoholism or substance abuse may be heightened with corroborating laboratory evidence (Table 13). Elevated mean corpuscular volume (MCV) and elevated liver function tests such as serum glutamic-oxaloacetic transaminase (SGOT), serum glutamic-pyruvic transaminase (SGPT), and lactate dehydrogenase (LDH) may be a sign of alcohol abuse. Elevated serum gamma-glutamyl transpeptidase (SGGT) is a particularly sensitive indicator of possible alcoholic liver disease. Decreased albumin, $B_{12}$, or folic acid may be evidence of prolonged malnutrition secondary to alcohol or substance abuse. Positive hepatitis B and HIV testing and bacteremia may indicate past or present iv use. Laboratory findings consistent with pancreatitis, hepatitis, bone marrow suppression, or certain types of infection may be clues to underlying alcoholism. Attempts are being made to develop laboratory profiles that will serve as better markers for early detection of alcohol problems. For example, the combination of gamma-glutamyl transferase (GGT) and MCV identifies 90 percent of alcoholics in the general medical population compared to 70 to 80 percent when MCV or GGT is used alone (2).

TABLE 13.  **Laboratory Findings Associated with Alcohol Abuse**

- Blood alcohol level
- Positive breathalyzer
- Elevated MCV
- Elevated SGOT, SGPT, LDH
- Elevated SGGT (particularly sensitive)
- Decreased albumin, $B_{12}$, folic acid
- Increased uric acid, elevated amylase, evidence of bone suppression

*Note.* MCV = mean corpuscular volume; SGOT = serum glutamic-oxaloacetic transaminase; SGPT = serum glutamic-pyruvic transaminase; LDH = lactate dehydrogenase; SGGT = serum gamma-glutamyl transpeptidase.

Unfortunately, these panels have unacceptable false negatives and positive results for clinical use at this time. The MCV is a measure of red blood cell size. Increased MCV ($>$95 cubic microns in males, 100 in females) is found with certain nutritional deficiencies (e.g., folate $B_{12}$) or can be associated with alcohol's direct effect on bone marrow cell production. Increased MCV is found in 45 to 90 percent of alcoholics, and only 1 to 5 percent of nonalcoholics demonstrate elevated MCVs (3).

GGT is a sensitive measure of liver enzyme induction. Greater than 70 percent of heavy drinkers have an elevated GGT ($>$40 units per liter). Drinking alcoholics have a four to 10 times higher rate of abnormal GGT than when they are abstinent. GGT as an indicator of heavy alcohol consumption has a sensitivity of 70 percent and a specificity of 90 percent. SGOT is elevated ($>$45 units per liter) in 30 to 60 percent of alcoholics, with a sensitivity of 80 percent. Irwin et al. reported preliminary evidence that increases of 20 percent for GGT and 50 percent for SGOT over baseline abstinence is a possible indicator for heavy drinking even if the increased values fall within the normal range and therefore may be an indicator of relapse (4). Liver, spleen scans, brain scans, and electroencephalogram (EEG) may be useful in the diagnosis.

## ■ DIAGNOSTIC INSTRUMENTS

Attempts at finding accurate psychological markers for the alcohol and substance abuser generally have failed. Early psychodynamic theorists described addictive behavior as related to oral regressive defense mechanisms. More recently, theorists have discussed ego disturbances, difficulty with affect regulation, and defective self-care mechanisms (5). Pathologic dependency and counterdependency and feelings of inadequacy and counterdependency feelings of bravado have been described in these patients.

Cognitive theorists have posited psychoactive substance abuse participation in tension and stress reduction, positive expectancy of mood elevation, and increased perception of self-adequacy (6). Additional psychiatric diagnoses have been described in 50 percent of alcoholics and cocaine abusers and up to 93 percent of iv heroin abusers. No one alcohol or substance abuse personality has proven to be etiologic. Vaillant's prospective study of college students with long-term follow-up has failed to identify an alcoholic personality predictive of substance abuse (7).

## *DIAGNOSTIC RESEARCH INSTRUMENTS*

The need for better standardized diagnostic research instruments in psychiatry has produced structured interviews that have been helpful in identifying alcoholism in large epidemiologic studies (7). These instruments are used also to identify other psychiatric diagnoses. The Schedule for Affective Disorders (SADS), based on the Research Diagnostic Criteria (RDC), is a forerunner to the Diagnostic Instrument Schedule (DIS). The DIS is based on DSM-III-R criteria and is designed as an instrument that can be given by trained lay interviewers. The Structured Clinical Interview for Diagnosis (SCID) is a more recent structured interview based on the DSM-III-R criteria that also has a capability to make DSM-III-R personality diagnoses. These instruments have proven to be fairly reliable in establishing DSM-III-R and RDC psychoactive substance abuse diagnoses. However, within this population, problems may exist in assessing other psychiatric diagnoses with these instruments. The anxiety, antisocial, and depression sections may be less useful in the psychoactive substance population.

There are several instruments designed for research purposes that finely measure attributes of alcohol abuse. The Alcohol Use Inventory (AUI) is a 17-item, self-administered, questionnaire instrument that reflects 1) perceived benefits of alcohol, 2) the problems concomitant to alcohol use, 3) disruptive consequences of drinking, and 4) the patient's concern about the use of alcohol and the extent to which the patient acknowledges having a drinking problem. The Alcohol Dependence Scale (ADS) is a brief 10-question instrument assessing physical dependence.

## DIMENSIONAL SCALES

Dimensional personality profile scales like the Minnesota Multiphasic Personality Inventory (MMPI) and the Symptom Checklist (SCL)-90 have been useful in substance abuse populations. In the hands of a skilled interpreter, common findings of elevated hysteria, paranoia, antisocial, and depression subscales can augment initial clinical impressions. A markedly elevated schizophrenia scale or evidence of male or female identity confusion may occasionally be expected. Valid profiles may indicate that the patient is dissimulating to fake good or bad. Although limited to augmentation of a good clinical diagnostic interview, the MMPI may be most useful to chart improvement over time. Due to the time-limited organic effects of alcohol, patients' symptoms frequently begin to clear after three or four weeks of abstinence, and this is reflected in the test (8). Personality subscales may improve as the acquired substance abuse-related personality attributes begin to clear. Conversely, serious psychiatric problems may also be unmasked following drug removal. Frequently, damage to personality structure improves, but recovery may not be total. The MacAndrews scale is a subset scale of MMPI that has been widely used for identifying alcoholics. The MacAndrews scale is a 48-question true-false scale that can correctly identify 82 percent of alcoholics. Although this scale has shown promise, recent studies have highlighted some of its limitations in the general medical population.

## DIAGNOSTIC SCREENING DEVICES

There are several instruments designed to measure various aspects of alcohol and other substance abuse. The majority of these instruments are not based on research criteria but have been found to be clinically useful in identifying psychoactive substance abuse. Two widely used alcoholism screening tests are the Michigan Alcoholism Screening Test (MAST) (Table 14) and the CAGE questionnaire (Table 15). These tests have the advantage of being self-administered, brief screens that can point the way for further study. The MAST is a 25-question form. The short MAST (SMAST) is a 13-item scale that correlates .90 with the MAST. The MAST has a test-retest reliability in excess of .85. The sensitivities of the MAST and of the SMAST are approximately .90 and .70, respectively. The proportion of nonalcoholics correctly identified as such averages .74 for the MAST. These tests screen for the major psychological, social, and physiologic consequences of alcoholism (9).

TABLE 14. **Michigan Alcoholism Screening Test (MAST)**

| Points | | | Yes | No |
|---|---|---|---|---|
| | 0. | Do you enjoy a drink now and then? | ___ | ___ |
| (2) | 1. | Do you feel you are a normal drinker? (By normal we mean you drink less than or as much as most other people.) | ___ | ___ |
| (2) | 2. | Have you ever awakened the morning after some drinking the night before and found that you could not remember a part of the evening? | ___ | ___ |
| (1) | 3. | Does your wife, husband, a parent, or other near relative ever worry or complain about your drinking? | ___ | ___ |
| (2) | 4. | Can you stop drinking without a struggle after one or two drinks? | ___ | ___ |
| (1) | 5. | Do you ever feel guilty about your drinking? | ___ | ___ |
| (2) | 6. | Do friends or relatives think you are a normal drinker? | ___ | ___ |

TABLE 14. **Michigan Alcoholism Screening Test (MAST) (*cont*)**

| Points | | | Yes | No |
|---|---|---|---|---|
| (0) | 7. | Do you ever try to limit your drinking to certain times of the day or to certain places? | ___ | ___ |
| (2) | 8. | Have you ever attended a meeting of Alcoholics Anonymous? | ___ | ___ |
| (1) | 9. | Have you gotten into physical fights when drinking? | ___ | ___ |
| (2) | 10. | Has your drinking ever created problems between you and your wife, husband, a parent, or other relative? | ___ | ___ |
| (2) | 11. | Has your wife, husband (or other family members) ever gone to anyone for help about your drinking? | ___ | ___ |
| (2) | 12. | Have you ever lost friends because of your drinking? | ___ | ___ |
| (2) | 13. | Have you ever gotten into trouble at work or school because of drinking? | ___ | ___ |
| (2) | 14. | Have you ever lost a job because of drinking? | ___ | ___ |
| (2) | 15. | Have you ever neglected your obligations, your family, or your work for two or more days in a row because you were drinking? | ___ | ___ |
| (1) | 16. | Do you drink before noon fairly often? | ___ | ___ |
| (2) | 17. | Have you ever been told you have liver trouble? Cirrhosis? | ___ | ___ |
| (2) | *18. | After heavy drinking have you ever had Delirium Tremens (D.T.'s) or severe shaking, or heard voices or seen things that really weren't there? | ___ | ___ |
| (5) | 19. | Have you ever gone to anyone for help about your drinking? | ___ | ___ |
| (5) | 20. | Have you ever been in a hospital because of drinking? | ___ | ___ |

TABLE 14. **Michigan Alcoholism Screening Test (MAST)** (*cont*)

| Points | | | Yes | No |
|---|---|---|---|---|
| (2) | 21. | Have you ever been a patient in a psychiatric hospital or on a psychiatric ward of a general hospital where drinking was part of the problem that resulted in hospitalization? | ___ | ___ |
| (2) | 22. | Have you ever been seen at a psychiatric or mental health clinic or gone to any doctor, social worker, or clergyman for help with any emotional problem, where drinking was part of the problem? | ___ | ___ |
| (2) | **23. | Have you ever been arrested for drunk driving, driving while intoxicated, or driving under the influence of alcoholic beverages? | ___ | ___ |
| | | (If YES, How many times? ___) | | |
| (2) | **24. | Have you ever been arrested, or taken into custody, even for a few hours, because of other drunk behavior? | ___ | ___ |
| | | (If YES, How many times? ___) | | |

*5 points for Delirium Tremens     **2 points for *each* arrest

*SCORING SYSTEM:* In general, five points or more would place the subject in an "alcoholic" category. Four points would suggest alcoholism, three points or less would indicate the subject was not alcoholic.

Programs using the above scoring system find it very sensitive at the five point level and it tends to find more people alcoholics than anticipated. However, it is a screening test and should be sensitive at its lower levels.

*Note.* Reprinted with permission from Selzer ML: The Michigan Alcoholism Screening Test: the quest for a new diagnostic instrument. Am J Psychiatry 1971; 127:1653–1658. Copyright © 1971 American Psychiatric Association.

## ADDICTION SEVERITY INDEX

The Addiction Severity Index (ASI) developed by McLellan et al. has proven to be a useful instrument in the psychoactive substance abuse population, particularly in treatment outcome research (10). The ASI establishes a scale and scoring system for

**TABLE 15.** **"CAGE" Screen for Diagnosis of Alcoholism**

| 2 or 3 = high index of suspicion | 4 = pathognomonic |
|---|---|

Have you ever:

C    thought you should CUT back on your drinking?

A    felt ANNOYED by people criticizing your drinking?

G    felt GUILTY or bad about your drinking?

E    had a morning EYE-OPENER to relieve hangover or nerves?

*Note.* Reproduced with permission from Ewing JA: Detecting alcoholism: the CAGE questionnaire. JAMA 1984; 252:1905–1907. Copyright © 1984 American Medical Association.

the severity of need for treatment in seven major areas: medical status, employment-support status, drug use, alcohol use, legal status, family-social relationships, and psychiatric status. This dimensional approach is most helpful in identifying treatment needs in attempting to match the patient with a specific tailored treatment. The instrument can be given by any trained person and will take approximately 50 to 60 minutes to administer.

## ■ REFERENCES

1. Gold MS, Dackis CA: Role of the laboratory in the evaluation of suspected drug abuse. J Clin Psychiatry 1986; 47:17–23
2. Lumeng L: New diagnostic markers of alcohol abuse. Hepatology 1986; 6:742–745
3. Watson RR, Mohs ME, Eskelson C, et al: Identification of alcohol abuse and alcoholism with biological parameters. Alcoholism: Clinical and Experimental Research 1986; 10:364–385
4. Irwin M, Baird S, Smith TL, et al: Use of laboratory tests to monitor heavy drinking. Am J Psychiatry 145:595–599, 1988
5. Helzer JE, Camino GJ, Hwu H, et al: Alcoholism: a cross-national comparison of population surveys with the DIS, in Alcoholism: A Medical Disorder. Edited by Rose RM, Barrett J. New York, Raven Press, 1986
6. Khantzian EJ: A clinical perspective of the cause-consequence controversy in alcoholic and addictive suffering. J Am Acad Psychoanal 1987; 15:521–537
7. Vaillant GE: The Natural History of Alcoholism. Cambridge, MA, Harvard University Press, 1983
8. Brown SA, Schuckit MA: Changes in depression among abstinent alcoholics. J Stud Alcohol 1988; 49:412–417

9. Schuckit MA: Alcoholism and other psychiatric disorders. Hosp Community Psychiatry 1983; 34:1022–1027
10. McLellan AT, Luborsky L, Woody GE, et al: Are the "addiction-related" problems of substance abusers really related? J Nerv Ment Dis 1981; 169:232–239

# CLINICAL FEATURES OF SUBSTANCE ABUSE 7

## ■ ALCOHOL

People vary a great deal in their tolerance to substances. In nonhabituated persons, blood alcohol levels (BALs) of 30 mg/100 ml can lead to mild attention problems and 50 mg/100 ml can cause mild coordination problems. Ataxia is present at 100 mg/100 ml. Confusion and decreased consciousness can occur at 200 mg/100 ml. BALs of 400 mg/100 ml may produce anesthesia, coma, and death. Body weight, speed of consumption, and food intake can influence BAL. The legal definition of impaired driving is 50 mg/100 ml; drunk driving is greater than 100 mg/100 ml.

Depending on the setting, intoxication can produce exhilaration, excitement, bravado, or depression, despondency, and suicidal ideation. Depression and despondency may increase with the chronicity of use. In addition to emotionality, personality changes, and loss of control, alcohol is a major contributor to physical assault, suicide, homicide, motor vehicle accidents, and other types of accidents. Individual and cultural variations of tolerance may influence the manifestation of symptoms. Alcohol can slow thinking and impair concentration, reasoning, attention, and judgment. Neuromuscular impairment can include slurred speech, poor motor performance, and ataxia.

## BLACKOUTS

Alcohol blackouts are transient episodes of amnesia that accompany varying degrees of intoxication. Generally, blackouts are symptomatic of alcoholism; however, they can occur rarely in individuals with social drinking patterns. The pathophysiology of blackouts is not well understood but may involve the interference of long-term memory storage, deep seizures, or, in some cases, psychological depression. In addition to total amnesia, alcohol can produce varying degrees of partial amnesia (1). These episodes need to be distinguished from loss of consciousness due to other causes. Orthostatic hypertension, seizure episodes, and simple loss of consciousness from excess alcohol sedation need to be ruled out. Often this confusion can be offset by careful interview.

## ALCOHOL IDIOSYNCRATIC INTOXICATION

Alcohol idiosyncratic intoxication or pathologic intoxication has been a controversial concept that is associated with blind, unfocused, destructive behavior during intoxication. This diagnosis should not be used indiscriminately. Simple alcohol intoxication can increase violent episodes in susceptible individuals and is generally correlated with BALs. Idiosyncratic intoxication can best be thought of as behavior that is not particularly goal directed and that occurs with small amounts of alcohol ingestion. When idiosyncratic intoxication is suspected, one should carefully rule out a seizure focus, organic brain syndromes, and antisocial or hysterical personalities. The workup should include a computed tomography (CT) scan of the head and electroencephalogram (EEG).

## NATURAL HISTORY

The signs and symptoms of alcoholism can be strikingly consistent among individuals in the late stages of the disease. There appear, however, to be subtypes of alcoholics that may present with different ages of onset, underlying etiologies, degrees of hereditary influence, social and cultural backgrounds, and natural outcomes.

Vaillant has conducted one of the few prospective longitudinal studies of alcoholics (2). Many alcoholics continued to drink until death, some stopped drinking, and others showed a pattern of long abstinence followed by relapses. Some medical personnel have an unduly pessimistic view of the natural course of alcoholism and believe alcoholics will not get better with or without treatment. Sometimes family members may have unrealistically hopeful wishes and believe that the alcoholic will stop drinking in the near future without help. Large-scale outcome studies suggest that approximately 30 percent of alcoholics will at some point in the course of their illness achieve stable abstinence without any form of treatment (3). This percentage improves in some studies to approximately 70 percent with some form of treatment. Treatment could include professional treatment and/or self-help groups. Vaillant also described a series of natural healing forces (e.g., church involvement, fear of medical complications, or fear of family loss) that may substitute for some aspects of formal treatment through the meeting of dependency needs.

## SUBTYPES

Jellinek was the first to describe subgroups of alcoholics, distinguishing individuals who had persistent alcohol-seeking behaviors and others who could abstain from alcohol for long periods of time, but quickly lost control and could not terminate intake after resumption of drinking (4). More recently, Cloninger et al. described two subtypes of alcoholics (5). Type 1 alcoholics generally start intake with heavy drinking reinforced by external circumstances after the age of 25; have greater ability to abstain for long periods of time; and frequently feel loss of control, guilt, and fear about their alcohol dependency. Type 2 alcoholics generally have an early onset before the age of 25 and show spontaneous alcohol-seeking behavior regardless of external circumstances. They have frequent fights and arrests and infrequently experience a feeling of a loss of control, guilt, or fear about alcohol dependency.

Several investigators have described a familial form of alcoholism. Those individuals with a positive family history of alcoholism have an earlier onset of problems, more antisocial features, more medical problems, and poor prognosis. In general, women have a later onset of problems, which may reflect different etiologic factors. Women have shown less hereditary transmission.

## MANY FACES OF ALCOHOLISM

It is important to understand alcoholism as a disease with many different patterns and characterized by relapses. An alcoholic may present as an elderly woman who begins drinking habitually after the death of her husband. Another example may be a surgeon who drinks alcoholically for a period of time, but when faced with the loss of her practice, receives treatment and recovers. Another example may be an individual with a job and family who loses everything due to drinking, becomes homeless for several years, and, through involvement with Alcoholics Anonymous (AA), regains his job and family. Some alcoholics never develop serious medical problems; the majority of alcoholics never seek treatment.

## MEDICAL COMPLICATIONS

Adverse physical effects of chronic alcohol abuse include organic mental disorders, diseases of the digestive tract (including liver disease, gastritis, ulcer, pancreatitis, and gastrointestinal cancers), bone marrow suppression, and muscular and hormonal changes. Alcohol appears to have direct toxic effects on the brain. This may combine with metabolic, traumatic, and nutritional deficits to cause the various alcohol-related organic mental disorders, discussed in Chapter 4. Alcohol intake can cause a progression of liver damage. Fatty liver develops in nearly anyone with sufficient alcohol intake. Serious alcoholic hepatitis, which can have up to a 50 percent five-year mortality rate, can develop. Liver cirrhosis occurs only in approximately 10 percent of alcoholics; however, 11,000 die from liver disease annually. Of patients with chronic pancreatitis, 75 percent have a diagnosis of alcoholism. Alcohol dissolves mucus and irritates gastric lining, contributing to bleeding. Every alcoholic should have a rectal exam with a stool guiac as part of a complete physical exam (6).

Alcohol, heavy tobacco use, and deficiencies of vitamins A and B all contribute to high cancer rates of the mouth, tongue, larynx, esophagus, stomach, liver, and pancreas. Patients with oral cancer (in which alcohol significantly contributes) tend to delay onset of treatment longer than most other cancer patients. Early detection is particularly crucial in these diseases.

Alcoholic cardiomyopathy can develop after 10 or more years of drinking. Abstinence contributes to recovery in those cases in which damage is not too extensive. Alcohol also has chronic effects on other muscle tissue.

## EFFECTS ON BLOOD

Alcoholism is part of the differential diagnosis for anemia, especially megaloblastic anemia. Due to reduced white cell count or further damage to immune functioning, the effects of continued heavy drinking on the possible progression and susceptibility to infection by human immunodeficiency virus (HIV) and progression to acquired immune deficiency syndrome (AIDS) are being studied. For similar reasons, other infectious diseases (e.g., tuberculosis and bacterial pneumonia) have been common in this group.

## EFFECTS ON HORMONES

Alcohol interferes with male sexual function and fertility directly through effects on testosterone levels and indirectly through testicular atrophy. Relatively increased levels of estrogen lead to developing gynecomastia and body hair loss. Sexual functioning is affected indirectly through alcohol's impact on the limbic system and the hypothalamic-pituitary axis (7). Alcohol may also impair parasympathetic nerve functioning, which may affect the ability to maintain an erection. Alcoholic peripheral neuropathy is characterized by a stocking-and-glove paresthesia, with decreased reflexes and autonomic nerve dysfunction causing impotence and orthostatic hypertension. This may be due to vitamin B deficiency or direct toxic effects of alcohol. In women there may be also severe gonadal failure, with an inability to produce adequate quantities of female hormones, affecting secondary sexual characteristics, reducing menstruation, and producing infertility.

## ADDITIONAL COMPLICATIONS

Alcoholism tends to increase blood pressure and is associated with increased risk of cerebrovascular accidents. Alcohol cerebellar degeneration is a slowly evolving condition encountered along with long-standing histories of excessive use. It affects the cerebellar cortex and produces truncal ataxia and gait disturbances. Central pontine myelinolysis is a rare neurologic condition of unknown etiology and high mortality. Also of unknown etiology, Marchiafava-Bignami disease is a rare demyelinating disease of the corpus callosum.

## ALCOHOL WITHDRAWAL SYMPTOMS

Alcohol withdrawal symptoms can occur after cessation of alcohol in chronic abuse or secondary to a relative drop in blood levels. Therefore, clearcut withdrawal symptoms may be present during a period of continuous alcohol consumption. Alcohol withdrawal proper precedes or accompanies more pathologic withdrawal phenomena such as delirium tremens (DTs), seizures, and alcohol hallucinosis. Increased duration of drinking and binge patterns of alcohol ingestion are clearly tied to an increase in withdrawal phenomena. By far, the most common and early symptoms are tremulousness, combined with general irritability, nausea, and vomiting occurring several hours after the last drink, frequently the next morning. The generalized tremor, which is coarse and of fast frequency (5 to 7 cycles per second), can worsen with motor activity or emotional stress; it is most likely observed when the hands or tongue are extended. Often patients complain only of feeling shaky inside. In addition, patients manifest malaise and autonomic hyperactivity, tachycardia, increased blood pressure, sweating, and orthostatic hypotension. Careful attention should be given to vital signs in a suspected alcoholic.

Peak symptoms occur 24 to 48 hours after the last drink in uncomplicated cases, and subside in five to seven days, even without treatment; mild irritability and insomnia may last 10 days or longer. It is helpful to educate patients about the time course of withdrawal because a rapid return to drinking may be precipitated by these residual withdrawal symptoms.

## ALCOHOL WITHDRAWAL SEIZURES

Seizures are associated with cessation of long-term use of alcohol. Most (90 percent) of these seizures occur seven to 38 hours after last use, with a peak incidence somewhat greater than 24 hours. Half of these occur in bursts of two to six grand mal seizures. Less than 3 percent develop status epilepticus, which can be a life-threatening condition unless interrupted. Focal seizures suggest a focal lesion, which may be the result of trauma or idiopathic epilepsy. Seizures can be precipitated by a short bout of drinking by lowering seizure threshold. These alcohol-precipitated seizures usually occur after a period of acute intoxication. Half of alcoholics experiencing seizures have been found to have abnormal CT scans (8). A careful neurologic examination may predict those who may need a CT scan. Positive focal neurologic signs have been found in 30 percent of those with a focal deficit on CT scan.

Hypomagnesemia, respiratory alkalosis, hypoglycemia, and increased intracellular sodium have been associated with alcohol seizures, and the seizures may be the result of hyperexcitability of the neuron systems caused by these conditions. Serum magnesium should be tested in alcoholic patients who develop seizures. These seizures have important prognostic value in predicting a complicated withdrawal period. Approximately one-third of patients with generalized seizures secondary to alcohol withdrawal go on to develop alcohol withdrawal DTs.

## ALCOHOL WITHDRAWAL DELIRIUM

DTs are distinguished from uncomplicated withdrawal symptoms by a characteristic delirium. Confusion, disorientation, fluctuating or clouded consciousness, and perceptual disturbances all may be present. The DTs have functioned as a prototype of all deliriums. The syndrome may include delusions, vivid hallucinations, agitation, insomnia, mild fever, and marked vital sign changes that can appear suddenly, but usually more gradually, two to three days after cessation of drinking, with peak intensity on the fourth to fifth day. Terror, agitation, and primarily visual hallucinations of insects, small animals, or perceptual distortions are classic, although a wide variation of presentations can occur.

The clinical picture can vary from quiet confusion, agitation, and peculiar behavior lasting several weeks to marked abnormal behavior, vivid terrifying delusions, and hallucinations. Hallucinations may be auditory and of a persecutory nature or they may be kinesthetic, such as tactile sensations of crawling insects. The level of consciousness may fluctuate widely. Approximately half of the cases present in an atypical manner. In most cases, DTs are benign and short lived. The delirium state may be characterized by several relapses separated by lucid intervals. The majority of cases subside after three days of full-blown DTs, although subacute symptom DTs may last as long as four to five weeks. With medical complications, it has been reported that up to 20 percent of cases may end fatally. Recent reports, however, have found an overall fatality rate that may be less than 1 percent. Deaths associated with DTs may relate to infections, fat emboli, or cardiac arrhythmia associated with hyperkalemia, hyperpyrexia, poor hydration, and hypertension. DTs generally occur in alcoholics with five to 15 years of heavy drinking who decrease their BALs or who have a major physical illness (e.g., infection, trauma, liver disease, metabolic disorders). Although only 1 to 2 percent of alcoholics who are hospitalized for detoxification develop DTs, the hospital setting can be important not only for the patient's comfort but for needed careful observation.

## ALCOHOL HALLUCINOSIS

Differential diagnosis of alcohol hallucinosis includes DTs, withdrawal syndrome, paranoid psychosis, and borderline transient psychotic episodes. In contrast to DTs, these hallucinations usually occur in a clear consciousness. Lack of autonomic symptoms also differentiate the syndrome from withdrawal syndromes. Hallucinations may range from sounds (e.g., clicks, roaring, humming, ringing bells, chanting) to frank voices of friends or enemies that are threatening or derogatory. A single derogatory remark may proceed to a relentless persistence of auditory accusations by several voices with auditory commands. Patients usually respond appropriately with fear, anxiety, and agitation. The symptoms may resemble paranoid schizophrenia. However, the diagnosis here is usually based on heavy alcohol use, lack of formal thought disorder, and lack of schizophrenic symptoms in the past or on family history. In the great majority of cases, the symptoms recede in a few hours to days, the patients fully realizing that the voices were imaginary. A small percentage of patients may proceed to develop a quiet, chronic, paranoid delusional state indistinguishable from frank schizophrenia. A period of six months has been reported as a cutoff point beyond which remission is not expected.

## ■ SEDATIVES, HYPNOTICS, AND ANXIOLYTICS

The course of central nervous system (CNS) abuse/dependence varies from long prodromal periods of use with benzodiazepines or hypnotics, more rapid onset of addiction with barbiturates, or episodic abuse with other CNS depressants like methaqualone (Quaalude) or ethchlorvynol (Placidyl). Combinations of CNS depressants with alcohol or with opiates can potentiate the level of intoxication, respiratory depression, and mortality.

Chronic sedative abuse can produce "blackouts" and neuropsychological damage similar to that experienced by alcoholics (9).

## ■ OPIOIDS

### *INTOXICATION AND WITHDRAWAL*

Intravenous (iv) heroin or opioid intoxication produces a subjective euphoric rush that can be highly reinforcing. Opioid users describe this feeling as a feeling of warmth, or an oceanic feeling. The daily use of opioids over days to weeks, depending on the dose and potency of the drug, will produce opioid withdrawal symptoms on cessation of use.

### *NEONATAL OPIOID WITHDRAWAL*

A syndrome of narcotic abstinence is reported in 60 to 94 percent of neonates of mothers addicted to opiates (10). Although the baby may appear normal at or shortly after birth, symptoms may appear 12 to 24 hours later, depending on the half-life of the opioid, and may persist for several months. The full-blown syndrome can include hyperactivity, tremors, seizures, hyperactive reflexes, gastrointestinal dysfunction, respiratory dysfunction, and vague autonomic symptoms (e.g., yawning, sneezing, sweating, nasal congestion, increased lacrimation, and fever). Long-term residual symptoms include infants appearing anxious, hard to please, hyperactive, and emotionally labile.

## ADVERSE PHYSICAL EFFECTS

Contaminated needles and impure drugs can lead to endocarditis, septicemia, pulmonary emboli, and pulmonary hypertension. Contaminants can cause skin infections, hepatitis B, and spread of HIV. Death rates in young addicts are increased 20-fold by infection, homicide, suicide, overdose, and (recently) AIDS. Opioid overdose should be suspected in any undiagnosed coma patient, especially along with respiratory depression, pupillary constriction, or presence of needle marks.

## PATHOPHYSIOLOGY

Basic research advances in identification of distinct subtypes of opioid receptors have provided increased understanding of the mechanism of cellular opioid neuroregulation and physiology. Cellular mechanisms of opioid receptors are being explored in relation to characteristics of opioid receptors and intracellular modulators of opioid action. Multiple subtypes of opioid receptors designated as mu, delta, kappa, sigma, and epsilon have been described. Neuroadaptation at receptor sites has been hypothesized to produce tolerance and dependence.

## PSYCHOSOCIAL FEATURES

Kandel and Faust extensively studied patterns of psychoactive substance abuse in adolescents and young adults and found a progression from tobacco, alcohol, and marijuana to sedatives, cocaine, and opioids (11). Regular marijuana use, depressive symptoms, lack of closeness to parents, and dropping out of school may predispose to later narcotic use. Often opioid abuse is endemic to communities that are economically disadvantaged with high unemployment, low family stability, increased tolerance of criminality, and increased hopelessness. These social stressors may result in hopelessness, low self-esteem, poor self-concept, and identification with drug-involved role models, and may be intervening variables in the increased opioid dependency rates in minorities. Where poverty and high unemployment are prevalent, many individuals may feel they have little to lose with drug experimentation, and conventional scare tactics have little impact. Alienation from social institutions such as school, increased social deviancy, and impulsivity are high-risk characteristics. There exists a clear association between heroin use and crime. The overwhelming majority of inner-city community members, however, are not opioid users. Research into the factors that are protective for individuals at risk is important.

## THE SELF-MEDICATION HYPOTHESIS

Khantzian found a strong interaction between dominant dysphoric feelings and drug preference (12). The self-medication hypothesis is that the individual self-selects drugs on the basis of personality and ego impairments. Khantzian emphasized an "antirage property to opioids" that provides a pharmacologic solution or defense against overwhelming anger that is due to either deficient ego defenses or low frustration tolerance. Patients may seek mastery over pain through self-administered drug titration of withdrawal and dysphoria.

## PROGRESSION

A course of heroin addiction generally involves a two- to six-year interval between regular heroin use and seeking of treatment. Early experimentation with opioids may not lead to opioid addiction, but once addiction develops, a life-long pattern of use and relapse frequently ensues. A preexisting personality disorder may be a factor for drug use progression. The need to secure the drug predisposes the addict to participate in illegal activities or complicates an already existing tendency toward criminality.

## ■ COCAINE

### INTOXICATION

The iv or free-base use greatly intensifies the rush. Tolerance to the euphoric effects develops during a binge; however, there is decreased tolerance for adverse experiences such as increasing anxiety, panic, or frank delirium. With prolonged cocaine administration, a transient delusional psychosis, simulating paranoid schizophrenia, can be seen. Usually the symptoms remit, although heavy prolonged use or predisposing psychopathology may result in persistence of psychosis. Generally higher dosages delineate overdose from simple intoxication. In humans, cocaine binges can last a few hours to several days, are highly reinforcing, and may lead to psychosis or death.

Cocaine (iv) half-life is less than 90 minutes, with euphoric effects lasting 15 to 20 minutes. Most cocaine is hydrolyzed in the body to benzoylecgonine, which may be detected in the urine up to 36 hours. Repeated dosages are self-administered in lines of 25 to 50 mg as rapid tolerance builds up to the euphoric effects. Smoked free-base cocaine has a rapid onset of intense euphoria within seconds because it passes directly from the lungs through the heart to the brain and does not have to pass the liver first. Euphoric effects depend on concentration and on the slope of the peak concentration (13).

## NATURAL COURSE

The majority of casual (especially intranasal) cocaine users do not become dependent, but the widespread thinking in the late 1970s that cocaine was not addictive was mistaken. The time lapse from first use to addiction is usually about four years with intranasal use in adults; however, it may be as little as one-and-a-half years in adolescents. With availability of more potent cocaine derivatives (e.g., "crack"), experimentation may result in presentation for treatment in months. In a random sample of 306 intranasal users in 1983, 90 percent reported adverse physical, psychological, social, and financial consequences and 65 percent reported using tranquilizers, alcohol, or heroin to counteract overstimulation or rebound dysphoria (14). Most cocaine addicts describe the initial experimentation with cocaine as being fun. At some point in the experience, cocaine use is no longer fun, but joyless and compulsive. The activating properties of the drug become more prominent as the euphoria wanes. Cocaine initially consumed in public places like bars and at parties may become an isolated, alienating experience, associated with considerable paranoia.

Because of the high cost of cocaine, financial and legal problems may be the first sign of trouble before other stigma of dependence develop. A loss of control, exaggerated involvement, and continued use despite adverse social, occupational, and health effects are criteria pointing to a diagnosis of cocaine dependency.

## ABSTINENCE SYMPTOMATOLOGY

Efforts have been made to study and correlate systematically abstinent phenomena with neurobiologic findings. Gawin and Kleber studied 30 chronic cocaine abusers with structured diagnostic interviews in a longitudinal fashion (15). They identified three phases of abstinent symptomatology with possible implications for intervention and future biologic research. Phase I is the immediate postuse cocaine dysphoria known as the "crash." During prolonged intoxication, subjects reported receiving diminished dysphoric effects from larger doses. Subsequent use served only to avoid the crash, consisting of depression, anhedonia, insomnia, anxiety, irritability, and intense cocaine craving. Major depressive features and suicidal ideation were prominent. Gradually, cocaine craving subsided and the desire for sleep superceded cocaine craving. Sedative agents such as benzodiazepines and alcohol can be used as self-medication in attempts to sleep. This partially explains the associated sedativism frequently found with cocaine dependence. Phase I can last up to three days.

In Phase II, low-level cocaine craving continues, with irritability, anxiety, and decreased capacity to experience pleasure. Over several days, the memory of the unpleasant cocaine effects wanes, some normalization returns, and craving for cocaine increases, especially in the context of environmental cues. Frequently, this leads to another binge cycle, which may repeat itself every three to 10 days. If the first two phases are successfully completed, a several-week third phase of milder episodic craving may develop in a context of conditioned and environmental stimuli. Many patients will appear to have a major depressive disorder shortly after cocaine bingeing and most of the symptoms will eventually clear.

## ADVERSE MEDICAL EFFECTS

Cocaine has been associated with acute and chronic ailments. Chronic intranasal use has led to nasoseptal defects due to vasoconstriction. Vasodilation also produces nasal stuffiness or "the runs." Anesthetic properties of cocaine may lead to oral numbness and dental neglect. Malnutrition, severe weight loss, and dehydration often result from cocaine binges. Cocaine (iv) use complicated by impurities may produce endocarditis, septicemia, HIV spread, local vasculitis, hepatitis B, emphysema, pulmonary emboli, and granulomas. Free-base cocaine has been associated with decreased pulmonary exchange, and pulmonary dysfunction may persist. Cocaine iv injection sites are characterized by prominent ecchymoses; opiate users more frequently show needle marks.

Positive cocaine urine test results have been found increasingly in homicide victims, in those arrested for murder, and in overdose deaths. Cocaine-induced fatalities have an average blood concentration of 6.2 mg/l (16). Congenital deficiency of pseudocholinesterase may slow down the metabolism and result in toxic levels, sudden delirium, and hypothermia. Deaths in recreational low-dose users have been reported. Acute agitation, diaphoresis, tachycardia, metabolic and respiratory acidosis, cardiac arrhythmia, and grand mal seizures can lead ultimately to respiratory arrest. Recurrent myocardial infarction in cocaine use associated with tachycardia and coronary vasoconstriction have been reported. Subarachnoid hemorrhage may be precipitated in patients with underlying arterial venous malformations.

Pregnant women who use cocaine may have increased risks for abruptio placenta, and babies from cocaine mothers have been shown to have decreased interactive behavior on Brazelton scales. Further research is being done to study the teratogenicity of cocaine in infants.

## ■ AMPHETAMINES

Amphetamine abuse may start in conjunction with weight loss treatment, energy enhancement, or more serious iv use. Amphetamine abuse by iv administration can present with the same medical complications as seen with iv cocaine or heroin. Amphetamines share many similar signs, symptoms, and long-term sequelae as cocaine.

# ■ PHENCYCLIDINE

Chronic psychotic episodes are reported following use of phencyclidine (PCP). With the unpredictability of the experience, it is difficult to explain the abuse of this substance in certain individuals. In contrast to the use of hallucinogens, use of PCP may lead to long-term neuropsychological deficits. PCP abuse may occur in conjunction with multiple substance abuse and may be associated with similar risk factors. Cases of pure PCP abuse have been reported, and in our experience these individuals appear to have significant psychopathology; however, it is difficult to distinguish drug effects from premorbid personality.

# ■ HALLUCINOGENS

Chronic use of hallucinogens has been noted to produce flashback experiences in 15–30 percent of chronic users, and prevalence of flashbacks increases with the number of times the individual seeks medical attention except during acute intoxication or disturbing flashbacks that may be precipitated by other substances such as marijuana. Recently, "designer drugs" such as methylene dioxyamphetamine (MDA) and methylene droxymethamphetamine (MDMA) (Ecstasy) have had popular use in college populations. The long term neuropsychological effect of these drugs in humans needs further study (17).

# ■ CANNABIS

Marijuana abuse tends to begin in adolescence. The use of liquor and cigarettes may be associated with marijuana abuse. Marijuana has also been described as a stepping stone to other illegal drugs. It is often used in combinations with other psychoactive substances (e.g., cocaine). Although many people experiment with marijuana, actual abuse patterns tend to be associated with introduction to drug youth subcultures, low parental monitoring, parental substance abuse, and abuse of drugs by peers. Marijuana abuse should be suspected in any teenager who has a characteristic set of symptoms, including 1) loss of communication with family, 2) erratic mood changes, 3) deterioration of moral values, 4) apathy, 5) change in friends, 6) truancy, 7) academic underachievement, 8) denial of use even when found with drug paraphernalia, and 9) obvious signs of intoxication (18) (Table 16).

## ADVERSE PSYCHOLOGICAL EFFECTS

Generally, the adverse effects of marijuana are not treated in the medical setting. Mild anxiety, depression, and paranoia are frequent occurrences. Several neuropsychological changes and deficits have been identified with marijuana intoxication. Decreases in complex reaction time tasks, digit code memory tasks, fine motor function, time estimation, the ability to track information over time, tactual form discrimination, and concept formation have been found. This translates into impairment in automobile driving, airplane flying, or any other complex motor skill. Difficulties in attention span, coordination, and depth perception

TABLE 16.   **Signs of Suspected Adolescent Drug Abuse**

- Drop in school performance
- Irritability
- Apathy
- Mood changes including depression
- Poor self-care
- Weight loss
- Oversensitivity with regards to questions about drinking or drugs
- Sudden changes in friends
- Loss of communication with family
- Obvious signs of intoxication
- Denial of use even when found with drug paraphernalia
- Deterioration of moral values
- Truancy

have been found up to 10 hours or more after use. Undesirable physical effects include conjunctivitis, dry mouth, and light-headedness. Emotional symptoms of anxiety, confusion, fear, and increased dependency can progress to panic or frank paranoid pathology. Marijuana can also exacerbate depression.

## CANNABIS PSYCHOSIS

Cannabis psychosis has been characterized by agitation, violence, and flight of ideas, with little thought disorder. Acute toxic psychosis has been described in chronic users and also in first-time users. Patients may present with a schizophrenic-like picture with first-rank psychotic symptoms. Cannabis psychosis, however, may be most linked with patients who have an underlying thought disorder. Marijuana has been found to be an independent variable for psychosis in previously well-controlled schizophrenics (19). Marijuana may distort the normal sense of reality and precipitate prolonged psychotic episodes.

## AMOTIVATIONAL SYNDROME

A chronic cannabis behavioral syndrome has been called amotivational syndrome (20). This controversial concept describes people who become passive and less goal directed and evidence decreased drive, memory, and problem-solving ability after chronic marijuana abuse. Fatigue, apathy, and what has been described as a "fog" can last for several weeks after cessation of use. This syndrome has been controversial due to methodological problems in the research. It has been described most frequently in third-world countries, where environmental factors or preexisting personality factors may play a large role.

## ADVERSE PHYSICAL EFFECTS

The long-term effects of chronic marijuana abuse are inconclusive. There is no convincing evidence that marijuana produces permanent changes in the brain. However, several biochemical findings have been reported. Marijuana has been studied in relationship to human male and female fertility, cell metabolism and protein synthesis, normal cell division, and spermatogenesis. Cannabis smoke contains carcinogens similar to tobacco, and chronic marijuana abuse may predispose to chronic obstructive lung disease and pulmonary neoplasm. Cannabis also increases heart rate and blood pressure, which may be crucial in patients with cardiovascular disease.

## ■ NICOTINE

### *INTOXICATION*

In chronic users, tobacco produces a calming euphoric effect. This effect is more pronounced after a period of abstinence; cigarette smokers frequently report that the first cigarette of the day is the most satisfying. Tolerance develops to the effect of nicotine. Nicotine has demonstrated all the classic signs and symptoms consistent with an addictive substance. Nicotine poisoning consists of nausea, salivation, abdominal pain, vomiting, diarrhea, headaches, dizziness, and cold sweat. Nicotine is a psychoactive substance, as evidenced by its euphoric effects and positive reinforcement patterns (21).

### *COURSE*

Tobacco addiction frequently presents as a relapsing condition similar to opioids or cocaine. Cigarette experimentation usually begins in the teenage years. Environmental influences are important; peer tobacco use, parental tobacco use, and use of other substances are contributing factors. Relapse may be evident during periods of high stress, anxiety or maladjustment, poor social support, or low confidence. There is a strong association between alcohol and smoking. Frequently alcoholics are able to stop drinking but have a lot of difficulty giving up smoking at the same time. Due to this experience, many alcoholic treatment programs essentially ignore the tobacco addiction.

Factors associated with poor long-term outcome consist of poor overall adjustment, poor social support, environmental stress, being around people that continue to smoke, being uninformed about the dangers of cigarette smoking, and having higher use or tolerance.

## NICOTINE WITHDRAWAL

Tobacco withdrawal is characterized by craving for a cigarette, irritability, anxiety, difficulty in concentration, and restlessness. Physical signs and symptoms include decreased heart rate, increased eating, increased sleep disturbance, and decreased alcohol intake. Higher nicotine tolerance correlates with severity of withdrawal symptoms.

## ADVERSE MEDICAL SEQUELAE

At this time, there are well-known associations between tobacco use and coronary vascular disease, chronic obstructive lung disease, lung cancer, oral cancers, and hypertension. Nicotine tends to increase liver drug metabolism and therefore may lower the levels of medications metabolized by the liver. Psychotropic medications, including neuroleptics and antidepressants, may have lower blood levels in smokers. Smoking is not recommended during pregnancy because smoking is associated with low birth weight.

## ■ INHALANTS

## COURSE

Inhalant users are predominantly socially economically deprived young males 13 to 15 years of age. American and Mexican Indians and teenagers in the southwest have been found to have a high prevalence. Amyl nitrite was popular in the 1970s in the homosexual population. Nitrous oxide may be prevalent among certain health personnel, especially dentists. Most users tend to cease the use after a relatively short period of time and may go on to abuse other psychoactive substances.

## ADVERSE MEDICAL EFFECTS

Deaths have been reported from central respiratory depression, cardiac arrhythmia, and accidents. Long-term damage to bone marrow, kidneys, liver, neuromuscular tissue, and brain have been reported.

## ■ REFERENCES

1. Frances RJ, Franklin JE: Alcohol-induced organic mental disorders, in The American Psychiatric Press Textbook of Neuropsychiatry. Edited by Hales RE, Yudofsky SC. Washington, DC, American Psychiatric Press, 1987

2. Vaillant GE: Natural history of male alcoholism. Arch Gen Psychiatry 39:127–133, 1982

3. Armor DJ, Polish SM, Stambul HB: Alcoholics and Treatment. New York, Wiley, 1978

4. Jellinek EM: The Disease Concept of Alcoholism. New Haven, CT, Hillhouse Press, 1960

5. Cloninger RC, Sigvardson S, Bohman M: Childhood personality predicts alcohol abuse in young adults. Alcoholism: Clinical and Experimental Research 1988; 12:494–505

6. Frances RJ: Signs and symptoms of alcoholism and substance abuse, in Textbook of Diagnostic Medicine: Psychiatric Problems. Edited by Samiy A, Gordon RD, Barondess J. 1987, pp 729–739

7. Van Thiel DH: Ethanol: its adverse effects upon the hypothalamic-pituitary-gonadal axis. Clin Med 1983; 101:21–33

8. Cala LA, Mastaglis FL: Computerized tomography in chronic alcoholics. Alcoholism (NY) 1981; 5:283–294

9. Bergman H, Borg S, Holm L: Neuropsychological impairment and the exclusive use of sedatives or hypnotics. Am J Psychiatry 37:215–217, 1980

10. Calabrese JR, Gulledge AD: The neonatal narcotic abstinence syndrome: a brief review. Can J Psychiatry 1985; 30:623–626

11. Kandel D, Faust R: Sequence and stages in patterns of adolescent drug use. Arch Gen Psychiatry 1975; 32:923–932

12. Khantzian EJ: The self-medication hypothesis of addictive disorders. Am J Psychiatry 1985; 142:1259–1264

13. Kleber HD, Gawin FH: The spectrum of cocaine abuse and its treatment. J Clin Psychiatry 1984; 45[12, section 2]:18–23

14. Washton AM, Gold MS, Pottash AC: Intranasal cocaine addiction. Lancet 1983; 2:1374

15. Gawin FH, Kleber HS: Abstinence symptomatology and psychiatric diagnosis in cocaine abusers. Arch Gen Psychiatry 1986; 43:107–113

16. Spiehler VR, Reed D: Brain concentrations of cocaine and benzoylecgonine in fatal cases. J Forensic Sci 1985; 30:1003–1011

17. Yager J, Crumpton E, Rubenstein R: Flashbacks among soldiers discharged as unfit who abused more than one drug. Am J Psychiatry 1983; 140;857–861

18. Niven RG: Adolescent drug abuse. Hosp Community Psychiatry 1986; 37:596–607

19. Talbott JA, Teague JW: Marijuana psychosis. JAMA 1969;
    210:299–302
20. Grinspoon L, Bakalar JB: Marihuana, in Substance Abuse: Clinical
    Problems and Perspectives. Edited by Lowinson JL, Ruiz P. Balti-
    more, Williams & Wilkins, 1981
21. Henningfield JE: Pharmacologic basis and treatment of cigarette
    smoking. J Clin Psychiatry 1984; 45:24–34

# TREATMENT APPROACHES TO ALCOHOLISM AND OTHER PSYCHOACTIVE SUBSTANCE USE DISORDERS  8

## ■ DIFFERENTIAL THERAPEUTICS

Choice of the right combination of treatments for addictive patients is still largely based on the conventional wisdom of clinical considerations rather than on experimentally proven indications, even though there has been a growth in addiction treatment outcome research. The choice of treatment or combination of treatments needs to take into account the fact that a majority of patients have an additional psychiatric illness, that multiple addiction is frequent, and that treatment selection should fit the specific needs of the patient on a case-by-case basis (1). Recent advances in the treatment of psychiatric disorders in terms of psychopharmacology, psychodynamically oriented treatment, cognitive- and behavioral-oriented individual approaches, and group and family treatment need to be incorporated in the choice of modality. Integration of Twelve-Step approaches such as Alcoholics Anonymous (AA), Substance Anonymous, and Narcotics Anonymous is also widely recommended. The following factors are important in considering choice of modality or combination of treatments: severity of medical and psychiatric illness, individual patient characteristics, cultural issues, finances, availability of treatment resources, and awareness of differential therapeutics of concomitant psychiatric disorders (2).

# ■ ABSTINENCE

A growing consensus of experts emphasizes the importance of complete abstinence from all psychoactive chemicals in the treatment of addictive disorders, except in cases where a replacement treatment is indicated (e.g., in the treatment of opioid addiction with methadone maintenance). Attempts aimed at controlled drinking as a goal of treatment have not identified subpopulations for which this is a viable option. Although every patient would like to continue alcohol use, it is impossible to identify patients with psychoactive substance use disorders for which controlled drinking is safe.

# ■ TREATMENT SETTING

## *INPATIENT*

Inpatient treatment for addictive patients is indicated in the presence of any of the following:

- Major medical and psychiatric problems and their complications
- Severe withdrawal such as delirium tremens (DTs) or seizures
- Failed attempt at outpatient treatment
- Family, friends, or AA members unavailable or unable to provide an adequate social support network for abstinence
- Polysubstance addiction requiring inpatient management

Trials of outpatient treatment are indicated before hospitalization unless there are counterindications. Patients prefer outpatient treatment, which is less disruptive and more cost effective than inpatient treatment. Inpatient detoxification can be followed by outpatient treatment or by inpatient rehabilitation. Choice of inpatient rehabilitation in a free-standing alcohol and drug treatment recovery program versus an inpatient psychiatric hospital versus a general psychiatric service depends on severity of additional psychiatric and medical problems. Patients with the most severe psychiatric illness may need to be treated on a general inpatient, locked psychiatric service before transfer to a mental illness, chemical abuse treatment unit (3).

## OUTPATIENT

Outpatient treatment delivery varies from the individual office practitioner to an addiction day or evening treatment program, which may utilize many techniques employed in inpatient treatment programs. Indications for outpatient alcohol detoxification include the following:

- High motivation and good social support
- No previous history of DTs or seizures
- Brief or not severe recent binges
- No severe medical or psychiatric problems or polyaddiction
- Previous successful outpatient detoxifications
- Daily visits over three to five days with a doctor are feasible
- Can be done in greater than 90 percent of cases

## ■ INTOXICATION

In most cases, simple intoxication does not come to medical attention. Patients with intoxication complicated by marked behavioral changes or obvious signs and symptoms of major medical complications may present to the emergency room for evaluation and treatment. These patients should be screened carefully for medical problems such as subdural hematomas, meningitis, acquired immune deficiency syndrome (AIDS) symptomatology, or endocarditis with embolization. General support measures include interrupting substance ingestion, providing a safe environment where the patient can be protected from self and others, decreasing sensory stimulation, and allowing the simple passage of time. A calm, nonthreatening manner should be employed, with reality orientation and clear communication. Attempts to reason extensively with most intoxicated patients will not be fruitful; in cases of hallucinogen abuse, however, individuals can frequently be "talked down" from pathologic intoxication.

## ALCOHOL

There is no proven amethystic agent that can hasten the cessation of alcohol intoxication. Conventional wisdom (i.e., that strong black coffee or cold showers promote sobriety) is erroneous. Several experimental approaches to delaying absorption or decreasing metabolism and elimination, such as environmental manipulation through lowering temperature and the use of electrolytes, have been tried. Opiate antagonists and central stimulants have also been studied. Naloxone, a narcotic antagonist, has been studied in regard to its reversal of alcohol-induced respiratory depression. Zimelidine and ibuprofen have been studied in terms of reducing alcohol cognitive impairments. Lithium has been studied in relationship to the attenuation of the subjective sense of intoxication. For practical purposes, however, safely allowing time to pass is the only effective measure to reverse acute intoxication.

## OPIOIDS

No specific measures are generally needed to treat opioid intoxication. If life-threatening overdose is suspected, prompt treatment with naloxone is necessary.

## COCAINE AND AMPHETAMINES

Cocaine abusers frequently self-medicate with central nervous system (CNS) depressants to antagonize the dysphoric stimulant properties of cocaine. In the acute medical setting of severe agitation, benzodiazepines such as diazepam or lorazepam may be a helpful adjunctive treatment. If frank psychosis persists, low-dose haloperidol (2 to 5 mg) may be helpful. Upward adjustment of dose may be necessary to control symptoms.

## PHENCYCLIDINE

Clinical signs and symptoms of phencyclidine (PCP) intoxication can range from mild symptoms that need no intervention to severe violent episodes that require police intervention. The general purpose is to prevent harm to self or others. Strong physical presence of at least five people is needed for physical containment (at least one person for each limb). Due to PCP's fat solubility, intoxication can last up to 30 days. Diazepam may be needed for the treatment of agitation, and neuroleptics such as haloperidol have been recommended for the treatment of PCP toxic psychosis.

## CANNABIS

Cannabis intoxication generally needs no formal treatment. Occasionally, severe anxiety attacks or acute paranoia develop. These episodes can generally be handled by reality orientation. Infrequently, severe anxiety may necessitate treatment with a benzodiazepine. In a case of cannabis psychosis, low-dose haloperidol may be helpful.

## HALLUCINOGENS

Hallucinogen intoxication rarely comes to medical attention. Generally these patients can be "talked down" with reality orientation and reassurance. More complicated situations exist when hallucinogens were taken inadvertently without the person's knowledge. A careful history and characteristic symptoms of hallucinogen use may help raise this possibility.

## INHALANTS

Inhalant intoxication can vary in its presentation and need for active treatment. The main principle is protection of the individual from harm and from harming others; symptoms are usually time limited.

## ■ OVERDOSE

There are more than 5 million poisonings each year. Emergency rooms may feel the burden of the care for these patients. Empathy with patients who repeatedly voluntarily overdose on various drugs can be difficult. Of patients who make it to an emergency room alive, less than 1 percent die (4). The emergency room becomes an important evaluation and triage center for substance-abusing patients.

## INITIAL ASSESSMENT AND TREATMENT

Because several drugs are slowly absorbed, the minimal time for observation of a suspected drug overdose should be four hours. Exact time of ingestion is often difficult to ascertain reliably. If there is good evidence that a specific drug was ingested, a call to the poison control center is suggested for treatment management, especially for those unfamiliar with drugs. The first crucial assessment is the adequacy of the airway, breathing, and cardiovascular perfusion, which includes assessment of airway patency, respiratory rate, blood pressure, and pulse. Securing a patient's airway by oral or nasal intubation or tracheostomy may be necessary. Ventilation manually or by machine may be necessary to regulate respiratory rate. Hypertension may be due to cardiac arrhythmias or alpha 2 blockade. Norepinephrine may be needed to maintain adequate perfusion. Every case of overdose with loss of consciousness or any case where the etiology of coma is unknown should receive 50 mg of dextrose 5% in water and 0.4 mg of naloxone, which may need to be repeated. Prompt response supports evidence for hypoglycemia, opiate overdose, or alcohol overdose. Dextrose 5% in water should not be given first in cases where Wernicke's encephalopathy is suspected because glucose can further suppress thiamine stores. Other basic support measures include diazepam treatment for status epilepticus and treatment of metabolic acidosis (5).

## ELIMINATION METHODS

Because gastric emptying is a technique for removal of toxic substances from the upper gastrointestinal tract before absorption, this technique is appropriate only for drugs orally ingested (6) (Table 17). One absolute counterindication is in cases of caustic ingestion.

### IPECAC SYRUP

Ipecac syrup induces vomiting in approximately 30 minutes. Ipecac syrup should be given only to patients who are awake and

TABLE 17. **Overdose Elimination Methods**

| | Ipecac Syrup | Forced Diuresis | Gastric Lavage | Activated Charcoal | Hemodialysis | Hemoperfusion |
|---|---|---|---|---|---|---|
| Acetaminophen | Yes | Yes (alkaline) | Yes | No | No | No |
| Alcohol | No | No | Yes | Yes | Yes | No |
| Amphetamine | Yes | Yes (acid) | Yes | Yes | Yes | |
| Barbiturates | | Only long | | Yes | | Yes |
| Benzodiazepines | Yes | No | Yes | Repeated | | |
| Carbon monoxide | No | No | No | No | No | No |
| Cocaine | No | No | No | No | No | No |
| Hypnotics | Yes | No | Yes | Yes | | |
| Hydrocarbons | Yes | | Yes | | | |
| Opioids | | | | | | |
| Phencyclidine | Only severe | Not with rhabdomyolysis (may precipitate renal failure) | Only severe | Yes | | |
| Phenothiazines | Yes | | Yes | Yes | | |
| Salicylates | Yes | Yes (alkaline) | Yes | Yes | Yes | |
| Tricyclics | | | | Repeated | No | No |

alert. Administration to other patients would risk aspiration. Ipecac syrup can be given anytime after ingestion and should be given even after spontaneous emesis because full gastric emptying may not have been accomplished. Ipecac syrup is generally given in doses of 30 ml in 500 ml of water.

## GASTRIC LAVAGE

Gastric lavage entails flushing the upper gastrointestinal system with water. This technique is attempted only on patients who are unconscious whose airway is secured by intubation; otherwise these patients would be at a high risk for aspiration. A large bore tube, generally Ewald 36F, is inserted into the stomach, and water is placed into the stomach and suctioned out. The distillate helps to remove contents from the stomach. No more than 300 ml should be used at any one time because more volume may actually force contents into the duodenum. This process should be repeated until the stomach content is clear.

## ACTIVATED CHARCOAL

Activated charcoal is placed in the stomach and serves as an absorbent to remove toxic substances. Activated charcoal has also been shown to reduce reabsorption of substances from the duodenum. Activated charcoal has been shown to be a very effective gastric emptying technique [7]. Again, intubation is needed to protect the airway. Activated charcoal is usually given in a dose of 500 to 1,000 g in 50 to 150 ml of 70 percent sorbitol.

## FORCED DIURESIS

When ingested substances are weak acids or bases, forced diuresis can be attempted in patients with functioning kidneys. The concept is to hasten the elimination of absorbed drugs by enhancing renal elimination. Forced alkaline diuresis is used with weak acids (e.g., aspirin). Renal elimination is increased by giving 1 ml/kg of sodium bicarbonate and lasix 3 to 6 ml/kg/hour. A urine pH of 7.5 to 7.9 should be achieved. Forced acid diuresis can be attempted with weak bases (e.g., PCP). Absorbic acid 1 to 2 g intravenous (iv) or orally every four hours is given along with lasix 3 to 6 ml/kg/hour in an attempt to lower the urine pH to 4.5 to 4.6.

## DIALYSIS

Dialysis is generally a heroic measure to save a life. Factors that influence success of dialysis are drugs that are 1) circulating in the plasma, 2) minimally bound to tissue, and 3) cleared poorly through the kidney. Poor renal clearance may be due to hypoperfusion or renal failure. This technique has been especially valuable with alcohol, amphetamine, and aspirin overdose.

## HYPOPERFUSION

Hypoperfusion is an extracorporeal blood-filtering technique like dialysis that uses a different type of membrane filtration. This technique has been especially useful in barbiturate overdose. Major complications include thrombocytopenia.

## TREATMENT OF OVERDOSES

Table 18 outlines the major medical complications and treatment approaches to various drug overdoses. Mortality with acetaminophen is 1 to 2 percent; complete recovery is generally within four days. Carbon monoxide poisoning symptoms range from headaches, dizziness, weakness, nausea, vomiting, and diminished visual acuity to tachycardia, tachypnea, ataxia, and seizures. Other manifestations include hemorrhages (cherry red spots on the skin), metabolic acidosis, coma, and death. Caustic acids tend to cause stomach erosion, and alkaline substances tend to cause esophageal necrosis, causing perforation acutely and strictures later. Cocaine overdose has been increasingly associated with death. Treatment of acidosis, seizures, and hypertension are imperative. Synthetic opioids such as propoxyphene (Darvon) may necessitate increased naloxone dose for reversal of CNS depression. Forced diuresis should not be attempted in cases of PCP overdose with suspected rhabdomyolysis. Acidification of the urine with ascorbic acid or ammonium chloride has been used alone and with lasix treatment. Phenothiazine overdose should be monitored for 48 hours for cardiac arrhythmia. Lidocaine may be necessary for treatment of cardiac arrhythmia, norepinephrine for hypotension, sodium bicarbonate for metabolic acidosis, and dilantin for seizures.

## ■ ALCOHOL WITHDRAWAL

## INPATIENT VERSUS OUTPATIENT SETTING

In cases of mild withdrawal, there is no need for pharmacologic intervention. Approximately 95 percent of patients have mild-to-moderate withdrawal symptoms. Supportive care without pharmacologic intervention is adequate for a significant number of patients. Even when pharmacologic intervention is needed, this can also be done as an outpatient. However, patients with organic brain syndrome, low intelligence, Wernicke's encephalopathy, de-

TABLE 18. **Management of Overdose**

| | Major Medical Complication | Antidote | Potentially Lethal Dose |
|---|---|---|---|
| Acetaminophen | Liver toxicity (peak, 72 to 96 hours) | Acetylcysteine 140 mg/kg p.o. followed by 70 mg/kg every four hours x 17 doses | 140 mg/kg |
| Alcohol | Respiratory depression | None | 350 to 700 mg/blood level |
| Amphetamine | Seizures | None | 20 to 25 mg/kg |
| Barbiturates short long | Respiratory depression | None | short >3 g long >6 g |
| Benzodiazepines | Sedation | None | |
| Carbon monoxide | Oxygen in tissue, neuropsychiatric sequelae | Hyperbaric oxygen | |
| Cocaine | Seizures, acidosis | None | |

| | | | |
|---|---|---|---|
| Hypnotics | Delirium, extrapyramidal side effects | None | May vary with tolerance |
| Hydrocarbons | Gastrointestinal, pulmonary, central nervous system side effects | None | |
| Opioids | Miosis, respiratory depression, decreased mental status | Naloxone 0.4 to 2 mg initially up to 10 mg (half-life 60 minutes) | May vary with tolerance |
| Phencyclidine | Hypertension, nystagmus, rhabdomyolysis | None | |
| Phenothiazines | Anticholinergic, extrapyramidal cardiac side effects | None | 150 mg/kg |
| Salicylates | Central nervous system side effects, acidosis | None | 500 mg/kg |
| Tricyclics | Cardiac side effects, hypotension, anticholinergic side effects | None | 35 mg/kg |

hydration, history of trauma, neurologic symptoms, medical complications, psychopathology that requires psychotropic medication, DTs, or alcoholic seizures or hallucinosis are probably best treated in an inpatient setting (Table 19). Polysubstance abuse and poor compliance are also indications for inpatient treatment. Poor family support, poor transportation, chaotic or unstable home environment, or environments where the patient is continually exposed to other alcohol and substance abusers are also poor prognostic signs for successful outpatient detoxification. The ad-

TABLE 19. **Medical Work-Up for Alcohol Withdrawal**

Medical History and Complete Physical Examination

Routine Laboratory Tests
- Complete blood count with differential
- Serum electrolytes
- Liver function tests (including bilirubin)
- Blood urea nitrogen
- Creatinine
- Fasting blood sugar
- Prothrombin time
- Cholesterol
- Triglycerides
- Calcium
- Magnesium
- Albumin with total protein
- Hepatitis B surface antigen
- B12 folic acid levels
- Stool guiac
- Urinalysis
- Urine drug and alcohol screen
- Chest X-ray, electrocardiogram

Ancillary Tests
- Electroencephalogram
- Head computed tomography
- Gastrointestinal series

*Note:* Reprinted with permission from Frances RJ, Franklin JE Jr: Alcohol and Other Psychoactive Substance Use Disorders, in *The American Psychiatric Press Textbook of Psychiatry.* Edited by Talbott JA, Hales RE, Yudofsky, SC. Washington, DC, American Psychiatric Press, 1988. Copyright © 1988 American Psychiatric Press.

vantages to outpatient detoxification are reducing costs, allowing the patient to continue to function in his or her environment, and providing a period of time for the therapist to evaluate the patient's motivation for treatment.

## PHARMACOLOGIC VERSUS
## NONPHARMACOLOGIC TREATMENT

Although the majority of alcohol patients who are seen in treatment will not get into major medical problems on alcohol withdrawal, the best approach should be conservative management. Prevention of DTs or alcoholic seizures should be a top priority. In addition to the patient's discomfort and the possibility of death, there is recent evidence that repeated uncontrolled alcohol withdrawal can hasten cognitive decline. Any patient with significant elevations of temperature, blood pressure, or respiratory rate; tremors; nausea or vomiting; a clear history of severe daily dependence or high tolerance; or a past history of DTs, seizures, or co-dependence on other CNS depressants should be detoxified pharmacologically. Patients who are experiencing medical complications such as infections, trauma, metabolic disorders, or liver disease should also be detoxified pharmacologically. Severe physical and subjective discomfort should be minimized. Pharmacologic detoxification can enhance compliance and provide an alcohol-free interval that may help the patient commit to treatment. There should be little concern in this setting of making the alcoholic a benzodiazepine abuser. Generally, there is no euphoria during detoxification. Negative countertransference feelings by staff members can result in withholding of appropriate medication. Medical personnel may be hardened by a patient with a long history of repeated alcohol detoxifications. The important thing to remember is that detoxification is just gradual withdrawal of the substance from the body.

The social model of detoxification generally preselects patients who have mild withdrawal symptoms or withdrawal history and mild-to-moderate dependence. Patients are housed in a supportive, safe environment for three or four days and detoxified without medication. Rest, vitamins, and regular meals help to structure and begin to help the patient to regulate his or her life again. These facilities should have adequate medical backup and provide close monitoring of patients for complications.

## PHARMACOLOGIC WITHDRAWAL

Whether the patient is an outpatient or an inpatient, careful monitoring of vital signs, physical signs, and subjective symptoms should be done routinely (see Table 19). Several objective rating scales are available to monitor the withdrawal state. The general principle of pharmacologic detoxification is substitution of a drug that is cross-tolerant with alcohol and slowly withdrawing it from the body. The primary goal is to prevent severe complications (e.g., seizures and DTs). Detoxification is also done to relieve patient discomfort. There are many agents that have shown some benefit for general sedation and diminishing of autonomic symptoms. Moskowitz et al.'s review of detoxification agents concluded that benzodiazepines are the only medications that consistently demonstrate, in controlled trials, superiority to placebos in treatment of withdrawal (8). The major advantages to benzodiazepines are that they are cross-tolerant to alcohol, which minimizes the onset of alcoholic seizures or DTs. If the patient is adequately covered with a benzodiazepine, complications of alcohol withdrawal are extremely rare. Benzodiazepines also have the advantage of having less respiratory depression and a good margin of safety between effective dose and overdose. Chlordiazepoxide (Librium) and diazepam (Valium) are relatively long-acting benzodiazepines and are most commonly used for detoxification. Intermediate benzodiazepines like lorazepam (Ativan) or oxazepam (Serax) have shorter half-lives and can be useful in patients whose liver metabolism is compromised due to liver damage or age. These medications decrease the risk of drug accumulation and overdose. Lorazepam has the added advantage of primarily renal clearance and reliable intramuscular (im) absorption.

## ■ DETOXIFICATION

Suppression of withdrawal symptoms is not a substitute for systematic withdrawal and detoxification. The conservative five-to seven-day regimen promotes comfort, decreases complications,

TABLE 20. **Standard Treatment Regimen for Alcohol Withdrawal**

**Outpatient**

Chlordiazepoxide 20 to 50 mg orally, four times on first day; 20 percent decrease in dose over a five-day period.

Daily visits to assess symptoms.

**Inpatient**

Chlordiazepoxide 25 to 100 mg orally four times on first day; 20 percent decrease in dose over five to seven days.

Chlordiazepoxide 25 to 100 mg orally every six hours in addition to standing dose as needed for agitation, tremors, or change in vital signs.

Thiamine 100 mg orally four times daily.

Folic acid 1 mg orally four times daily.

Multivitamin one per day.

Magnesium sulfate 1 g im every six hours for two days (if status postwithdrawal seizures).

*Note:* Reprinted with permission from Frances RJ, Franklin JE Jr: Alcohol and Other Psychoactive Substance Use Disorders, in *The American Psychiatric Press Textbook of Psychiatry.* Edited by Talbott JA, Hales RE, Yudofsky, SC. Washington, DC, American Psychiatric Press, 1988. Copyright © 1988 American Psychiatric Press.

provides structure, and may help the patient cope cognitively and emotionally with the initial phases of treatment (Table 20).

Outpatient detoxification for alcoholism can be accomplished with chlordiazepine 25 mg qid decreasing to zero within four to five days along with thiamine 50 to 100 mg orally or im, multivitamins, and folic acid 1 to 3 mg/day (9). When indicated, disulfiram (Antabuse) can be added after physical examination, electrocardiogram, and blood work are completed and greater than 72 hours after the patient has stopped drinking, in the absence of counterindications such as cardiac arrhythmias, heart disease, severe liver disease, esophageal varices, pregnancy, or seizure disorder. Inpatient withdrawal from alcohol is accomplished with chlordiazepoxide (Librium) orally 25 to 100 mg qid with 25 to 50 mg every two hours prn for positive withdrawal signs. Doses can be held if the patient appears intoxicated. A history of withdrawal seizures may indicate a need for magnesium sulfate 1 g four times a day for two days. Thiamine 100 mg orally or im, folic acid 1 to 3 mg, and multivitamins should also be added.

## OTHER CNS DEPRESSANTS

Withdrawal of other CNS depressants such as benzodiazepines or barbiturates can necessitate pharmacologic withdrawal. Benzodiazepines in high doses for short periods of time or lower to moderate dosages for long periods of time (i.e., months, years) require some form of detoxification. Even a low dose of diazepam (i.e., 5 to 10 mg) prescribed over a period of months or years can result in significant withdrawal symptoms (e.g., anxiety, insomnia, seizures) on abrupt cessation of use. Conservative detoxification requires a slow withdrawal over several days or weeks. Benzodiazepine abuse can reach several hundred milligrams of diazepam or its equivalent. Individuals who can tolerate these extremely high dosages are dependent and require pharmacologic detoxification with active substance abuse treatment. Seizures are often the first sign of benzodiazepine withdrawal or a sign of inadequate coverage. Benzodiazepines generally can be substituted with chlordiazepoxide or diazepam (long half-life) for detoxification purposes. The standard benzodiazepine detoxification regimen is outlined in Table 21. Benzodiazepine detoxification is best attempted in an inpatient setting.

Alprazolam (Xanax), a relatively new benzodiazepine, appears to have some unique properties that make it less amenable to drug substitution. Breakthrough seizures have been reported despite adequate detoxification with chlordiazepoxide. Alprazolam detoxification should include an estimation of daily use or abuse and a slow withdrawal with alprazolam over a several-week period. Clonazepam (Klonipin) has also been successfully used in alprazolam detoxification.

If the patient is unreliable or the amount of daily abuse is difficult to ascertain, a pentobarbital challenge test can be used to estimate the starting dose (Table 22).

CNS depressants like glutethimide (Doriden) are generally used in an episodic fashion and do not require formal detoxification. Other CNS depressants like barbiturates or methaqualone

TABLE 21.  **Benzodiazepine Detoxification**

1. Estimate usual maintenance dose by history or pentobarbital challenge test (see Table 22).

2. Divide maintenance dose into equivalent quarterly doses of diazepam and administer first two days.

3. Decrease diazepam 10 percent per day.

4. Administer diazepam 5 mg orally every six hours in addition as needed for signs of increased withdrawal (increased pulse, increased blood pressure, diaphoresis).

5. When the diazepam dose approaches 10 percent, reduce dose slowly over three to four days and discontinue.

*Note.* Adapted from Frances RJ, Franklin JE Jr: Alcohol and Other Psychoactive Substance Use Disorders, in *The American Psychiatric Press Textbook of Psychiatry.* Edited by Talbott JA, Hales RE, Yudofsky, SC. Washington, DC, American Psychiatric Press, 1988. Copyright © 1988 American Psychiatric Press.

TABLE 22.  **Pentobarbital Challenge Test: Clinical Responses to 200-mg Test Dose of Pentobarbital**

| Patient's Condition After Test Dose | Degree of Tolerance | Estimated 24-Hour Pentobarbital Requirement (mg) |
| --- | --- | --- |
| Asleep, but arousal | None or minimal | None |
| Drowsy; slurred speech; ataxia; marked intoxication | Definite but mild | 400 to 600 |
| Comfortable; fine lateral nystagmus is only sign of intoxication | Marked | 600 to 1,000 |
| No signs of drug effect; abstinence signs may persist | Extreme | 1,000 to 1,200 or more |

*Note.* Adapted from Smith DE, Wesson DR: Phenobarbital technique for treatment of barbiturate dependence. Arch Gen Psychiatry 1971; 24:56–60. Copyright © 1971 American Medical Association.

(Quaalude) can be abused on a chronic basis and require detoxification. Barbiturates can be detoxified by using a long-acting benzodiazepine or a long-acting barbiturate, such as phenobarbital.

## OPIATES

Opiate detoxification may be needed to interrupt an addictive pattern to illegal or legal opiates. Heroin, morphine, codeine, demerol, and other various synthetic opiate drugs may require detoxification. More often these patients do not present for formal detoxification. Cessation of use may coincide with an interruption of supply, imprisonment, or a regimen of self-detoxification. Methadone detoxification can prove to be difficult due to its long half-life and long periods of use (9).

One approach to detoxification is using the abused opioid and slowly tapering it over a period of time. Although this is an untenable approach to illegal drugs like heroin, codeine, for example, could be detoxified in this manner. An estimation of the milligrams of total daily use is obtained. This amount is mixed with 30 mg of cherry syrup. The amount of codeine in the solution is slowly decreased over a 10-day period. A low dose (25 to 50 mg) of thioridazine (Mellaril) concentrate can be added to decrease subjective discomfort.

Another major approach is to substitute a long-acting opioid like methadone and decrease it over a 14-day period. An equivalent dose of methadone is substituted for the abused opioid (i.e., heroin). For most heroin addicts, 20 mg of methadone covers initial symptoms. The methadone should be decreased slowly over a 14-day period.

Clonidine is an alpha 2 agonist that has been shown effectively to suppress signs and symptoms of autonomic sympathetic activation during withdrawal. Opioid receptors have been found to be associated with the locus ceruleus (LC) area of the brain stem. The LC is a major supplier of norepinephrine to the rest of the brain and is instrumental in autonomic arousal during opioid withdrawal. Chronic opioid use suppresses LC function; cessation of use causes a rebound activation of the autonomic sympathetic system. Based on this principle, clonidine has been used during opiate detoxification. Clinically, clonidine is generally effective at suppressing autonomic signs and symptoms of withdrawal. It has been less successful in decreasing the subjective discomfort of withdrawal. Clonidine detoxification success increases with mild dependence, higher motivation, and inpatient status. Clonidine is given orally on the first day in a range of 0.1 to 0.3 mg three times a day and increased on the third day to 0.4 to 0.7 mg three times a day for a total detoxification of 10 to 14 days. In appropriate patients, naltrexone can be started during the clonidine detoxification. The major side effects of clonidine administration are hypotension and sedation (Table 23).

## NALTREXONE TREATMENT

Naltrexone is an opioid antagonist and blocks opioid receptors. Clinically, it has been used to serve as a deterrent to continued opioid use. Its long-term use results in gradual extinction of drug-seeking behavior and appears to be a valuable tool in abstinence-oriented treatment. Naltrexone is usually given as a 25 to 50 mg daily dose over the initial five- to 10-day period, then gradually increased to 100 to 150 mg three times a week. High refusal and drop-out rates have limited the use of naltrexone to highly motivated individuals with a good prognosis who are likely to do well in a variety of treatment options.

TABLE 23. **Opiate Detoxification**

### Methadone

Outpatient: Decrease methadone 10 percent per week until 10- to 20-mg range, then decrease 3 percent per week.

Inpatient: Decrease 1 mg/day over 20 days; can be done more rapidly if necessary.

### Clonidine

After patient stabilized at 20 mg of methadone, can abruptly switch to clonidine 0.1 to 0.3 mg three times daily for two days, then third day 0.2 to 0.7 mg three times daily for eight to 14 days, then discontinue.

*Note.* Adapted from Frances RJ, Franklin JE Jr: Alcohol and Other Psychoactive Substance Use Disorders, in *The American Psychiatric Press Textbook of Psychiatry.* Edited by Talbott JA, Hales RE, Yudofsky, SC. Washington, DC, American Psychiatric Press, 1988. Copyright © 1988 American Psychiatric Press.

## METHADONE MAINTENANCE

Methadone maintenance is an attempt to interrupt a drug addict's life-style, to promote stability and employment, and to decrease criminal activity. Most methadone patients are on a regimen that is indeterminate in length. Stable methadone maintenance may also reduce iv drug abuse and AIDS risk.

Methadone is a relatively long-acting (half-life of 24 to 36 hours) cross-tolerant opioid that mutes extreme fluctuation in opioid blood level and blunts euphoric response to illicit heroin. Methadone can be administered once daily and provides a treatment structure for rehabilitation. Although a mainstay treatment, only 20 to 25 percent of addicts receive this treatment. It is primarily indicated for the hard-core addict. Starting doses are usually 20 to 40 mg, depending on degree of dependence, and may necessitate an upward increase to 120 mg/day. Narcotics Anonymous (NA)-oriented rehabilitation programs or therapeutic communities may exclude patients on methadone. Although controversy continues to surround the drug substitution model, it cannot diminish the very positive therapeutic effects of methadone in a subset of patients.

A number of patients who have successfully interrupted their drug life-style should be considered for methadone detoxification. Often detoxification is at the request of the patient. Many individuals have been on methadone for several years. When indicated, methadone should be withdrawn slowly to minimize discomfort; this is often a protracted affair. In methadone programs, the medication ideally should not be decreased more than 10 percent per week. Below 10 to 20 mg of methadone, subjective symptoms of withdrawal may intensify and necessitate a further decrease in the rate of withdrawal to 3 percent per week.

Many addicts have compromised liver function due to alcohol abuse or hepatitis. Methadone use may be contraindicated with severe liver damage.

L-alpha acetyl methadol (LAAM) is a long-acting opioid agonist and is used in a similar fashion as methadone for narcotic maintenance. It has a longer half-life and thus may have the advantage of having to be taken only three times a week. Buprenorphine (Buprenex) is a mixed agonist-antagonist that has also been used in experimental settings and has lower addictive properties. These drugs may have some future role in substance abuse treatment but are not appropriate for general clinical use at this time.

## COCAINE, CANNABIS, HALLUCINOGENS, AND INHALANTS

There are no specific pharmacologic detoxification regimens for these substances. General support measures are usually adequate.

## ■ POLYSUBSTANCE ABUSE

### DETOXIFICATION

Polysubstance abuse also poses problems with detoxification. Withdrawal with multiple substances at once can be confusing and cause the misinterpretation of withdrawal symptoms. When alcohol or benzodiazepine detoxification is needed in addition to opioid detoxification, alcohol or benzodiazepine detoxification should be attempted first due to the life-threatening nature of CNS depressant withdrawal and the length of opiate detoxification. Combined detoxification from different drug classes simultaneously can greatly increase a patient's physical or psychological discomfort and lead to higher elopement or relapse. Greater risk of iatrogenic overdose exists with combinations of benzodiazepines and methadone, requiring close patient monitoring and adjusting doses as needed.

### INTEGRATING TREATMENT APPROACHES

The problem and magnitude of polysubstance abuse has not been adequately addressed by the treatment system. Frequently, drug and alcohol programs are separately funded. Often alcohol counselors lack training or are not motivated to treat the polysubstance abuse population. Certified alcoholism counselor (CAC) training programs should require ongoing education concerning the latest treatment approaches with drug-abusing clientele. Until recently, many AA groups were having difficulty integrating younger polysubstance abusers into their membership.

Unfortunately, a "my addiction is better than your addiction" attitude can develop. These attitudes in clinical treatment settings must be confronted with education and with greater tolerance of demographic differences between different substance abuse populations. The middle-aged white male exclusively an alcoholic, once common in treatment facilities, is outnumbered by a younger, polyaddicted, and more heterogeneous population with frequent additional psychiatric problems.

## ■ REHABILITATION

The rehabilitation model of treatment (Table 24), which was pioneered in alcohol and drug abuse, has become an important model for a variety of categories of psychiatric illness. It includes

TABLE 24. **Inpatient Treatment Rehabilitation Modalities for Psychoactive Substance Abuse Disorders**

- Diagnostic evaluation
- Drug-free periods
- Medication trials
- Team approach
- Group therapy
- Psychoeducation
- Family evaluation and treatment
- Twelve-Step programs (e.g., Alcoholics Anonymous, Narcotics Anonymous)
- Individual counseling
- Activity therapy
- Urine testing-abstinence orientation
- Discharge planning
- Follow-up treatment

*Note.* Adapted from Frances RJ, Franklin JE Jr: Alcohol and Other Psychoactive Substance Use Disorders, in *The American Psychiatric Press Textbook of Psychiatry.* Edited by Talbott JA, Hales RE, Yudofsky, SC. Washington, DC, American Psychiatric Press, 1988. Copyright © 1988 American Psychiatric Press.

combinations of self-help, counseling, psychoeducation to patients and families, relapse prevention, group treatment, the use of a warm supportive environment, and emphasis on a medical model geared to reducing stigma and blame. Most treatment units are highly structured, insist on an abstinence goal, and utilize lectures, films, and discussion groups as part of a complete cognitive and educational program. Patients are frequently converted into active Twelve-Step members and are encouraged to continue in aftercare.

A highly skilled professional team with ready availability of consultation is needed to integrate counseling, cognitive and behavioral treatment, relapse prevention strategies, interpersonal therapy, family therapy, group treatment, applied psychodynamically oriented psychotherapy, brief psychodynamically oriented psychotherapy, social network approaches, counseling, psychoeducation, and occupational and recreational therapy. Most inpatient programs include five to seven days for detoxification and three to six weeks for rehabilitation, depending on patient needs. Longer stays are indicated for patients with greater severity of illness or dual diagnoses, for adolescents, and for patients with severe medical problems.

The rehabilitation model emphasizes providing opportunities for patients to practice social skills, gain control over impulses, and use the highly structured program as an auxiliary superego, and encourages self-honesty and expression of feelings. The program promotes the use of higher-level defenses (e.g., intellectualization and reaction formation) and actively confronts more primitive defenses (e.g., denial, splitting, and projection), especially when these defenses are used in relationship to the issue of abstinence (10).

## REHABILITATION SETTINGS

Rehabilitation can take place in free-standing rehabilitation programs, MICA (mental illness, chemical abuse) units, general hospitals, inpatient programs, organized outpatient day and evening hospitals, therapeutic communities, and halfway houses. Addiction day treatment programs utilize many of the same techniques employed in inpatient treatment programs. They are staffed by interdisciplinary teams, including drug addiction counselors, who develop an individualized treatment plan. Organized outpatient alcohol programs may provide anywhere from several hours of individual, family, group, and psychoeducational treatment per week to a full-service day or evening hospital program. These programs are less restrictive and provide an alternative to hospitalization and may be useful as part of an aftercare program.

## AFTERCARE

Discharge from an inpatient or organized outpatient program requires consideration of aftercare as part of the treatment plan. Referral to a Twelve-Step program is frequently complementary to other therapeutic interventions, although self-help programs may be sufficient for some people when attended faithfully. Long-term follow-up care for at least two years after start of abstinence is usually recommended.

## ■ MODALITIES OF TREATMENT

## INDIVIDUAL THERAPY

Individual therapy can be conducted alone or in conjunction with other modalities, including pharmacotherapy, Twelve-Step programs, and family and group treatments. Abstinence is an important parameter of effective individual treatment and should be considered both a goal and a means to treatment success. Treatments range from psychodynamically informed supportive and expressive treatment to cognitive, behaviorally oriented treatment. Individual treatments are especially indicated when patients face bereavement, loss, or social disruption and have targeted problems (e.g., anxiety disorders or panic disorders). Patients with anxiety disorders especially benefit from cognitive, behaviorally oriented treatment (11).

### PSYCHODYNAMICALLY ORIENTED THERAPY

Psychodynamically oriented individual treatment works best for patients with problems in identity, separation and individuation, affect regulation, self-governance, and self-care. The following indications for psychodynamically oriented therapy are true for those patients who have addictive disorders in addition to other neurotic problems: 1) psychological mindedness; 2) capacity for honesty, intimacy, and identification with the therapist; 3) average to superior intelligence; 4) economic stability; 5) high motivation; and 6) a willingness to discuss conflict. In these patients, expressive psychotherapy may lead to deepening of a capacity to tolerate depression and anxiety without using substances. When patients are not abstinent, exploratory treatment may do more harm than good, with reactivation of painful conflicts leading to further drinking and regression.

Formal psychoanalysis is counterindicated in the early phases of addictive treatment, especially in those who are actively drinking. With abstinence, however, a select subgroup responds well to insight-oriented psychotherapy.

### INITIATING INDIVIDUAL TREATMENT: THE THERAPEUTIC CONTRACT

At the outset, the therapist should concentrate on how the patient can accept having a problem and the need for treatment in order to achieve and maintain sobriety. A therapeutic contract with the patient should include agreement about frequency and treatment modality or combination, limit-setting regarding the continuation of treatment in the face of continued use of substances, agreement to include involving important significant others in the social network, a clear goal of abstinence, psychopharmacologic treatment (e.g., disulfiram) if indicated, and arrangements regarding fee and time. Individual therapy may also be the treatment of choice in the management of a large number of psychiatric disorders that may coexist with alcohol addiction. Depending on treatment indications, appropriate pharmacologic treatment of patients with dual diagnoses will also need to be considered (12).

## GROUP THERAPY

Group therapy is frequently the principal inpatient and outpatient treatment modality for addictive disorders. Groups provide opportunities for resocialization, practicing of social skills and object relatedness, and impulse control; they also foster an identity as a recovering person (13). They support acceptance of abstinence and provide support for self-esteem and reality testing. Groups for addictive patients have the advantage of providing a homogeneous issue of dealing with addictions as a jump-off point to discussing other problems that may be shared.

A variety of group formats have been found useful including assertiveness training groups; marital couples groups; and groups for self-control, for ego strength, for self-concept, and for mood problems (e.g., anxiety and depression). Groups consisting of six to 10 members may provide opportunity for discussion, education about chemical abuse, and models of different stages of sobriety. Groups may be used to help in problem solving, may focus on specific behavioral problems, and may help the patient realize that others share similar problems. They may be psychodynamically oriented, confrontational, or problem solving; they may offer couples and marital therapy or occupational counseling. Addiction treatment programs frequently employ orientation didactic groups, which may aid retention in treatment, promote cohesiveness, and support acceptance of longer-term rehabilitation.

## PSYCHOPHARMACOLOGY

In the treatment of psychoactive substance use disorders, medications may be prescribed for detoxification, treatment of co-morbid psychiatric disorders, complicating neuropsychological and medical disorders, attenuation of craving or euphoria, or psychological ego support (e.g., disulfiram in alcoholics). Generally, these medications are used as adjuncts to psychosocial treatment and education. Physicians should have a clear understanding of differential diagnosis and natural history of substance abuse disorders, the limitations of medications, drug-drug interactions, and side effects.

### DISULFIRAM

Disulfiram (Antabuse) is a medication adjunct in the treatment of recovering alcoholics. Disulfiram is used to enhance motivation for continued abstinence by discouraging impulsive alcohol use. Disulfiram is a potent reversible aldehyde dehydrogenase inhibitor. Aldehyde dehydrogenase is an enzyme that metabolizes acetaldehyde, the first metabolite of alcohol. Inhibition of this step produces a buildup of acetaldehyde, which results in toxicity. Clinically, this disulfiram-alcohol reaction consists of symptoms including nausea, vomiting, cramps, flushing, and vasomotor collapse. Disulfiram also appears to have a catecholamine effect, which may contribute to the alcohol reaction and make its use counterindicated with monoamine oxidase (MAO) inhibitor use. Other counterindications include the presence of medical conditions that would be greatly exacerbated by a disulfiram-alcohol reaction, including liver disease, esophageal varices, heart disease, heart failure, emphysema, and peptic ulcer disease. It should not be used in patients likely to become pregnant. Psychiatric counterindications include psychosis and severe depression. Disulfiram can exacerbate psychosis. Severely depressed suicidal patients may purposely precipitate a disulfiram reaction.

Treatment facilities vary in their use and attitudes toward disulfiram. Some AA-oriented programs may discourage the use of any medication and see disulfiram as an unnecessary psychopharmacologic crutch. Many programs use disulfiram as an adjunctive tool in promoting abstinence. Although there has not been convincing evidence that disulfiram use affects long-term outcomes globally, disulfiram has been shown to be useful in certain subtypes. Older, socially stable alcoholics and affluent, married, less sociopathic patients who tend to be compulsive do better on disulfiram.

Disulfiram has relatively mild side effects, including sedation, halitosis, skin rash, and temporary impotence. More serious side effects include peripheral neuropathy, seizures, optic neuritis, or psychosis and occur rarely.

Initial starting doses of disulfiram are 250 to 500 mg/day. It can be administered in an oral suspension. Subcutaneous implantation has been used experimentally but is not clinically available. Dosages can be adjusted downward to 125 mg if sedation or other side effects are excessive or in those with relative counterindications. Patients should be fully informed about the rationale of disulfiram use, the disulfiram-alcohol reaction, and common side effects.

## LITHIUM

Lithium is an integral component of the treatment of psychoactive substance abusers with underlying primary bipolar or cyclothymic disorders. Lithium treatment may mute or abort extreme mood swings or indirectly affect psychoactive substance abuse intake. Mania or hypomania is associated with increased alcohol or cocaine use. Lithium-responsive depression may also be associated with cocaine or alcohol abuse. Lithium has also been associated with decreased subjective experience of intoxication, antagonization of deficits in cognitive and motor function during intoxication, and reduced alcohol consumption. Improved outcome has been demonstrated in nondepressed, primary alcoholics treated with maintenance lithium. These findings, however, are preliminary and there is not enough evidence to make the case for the use of lithium in primary alcoholics without an affective disorder (14). In addition, caution should be exercised in prescribing lithium to individuals who are actively abusing substances or to individuals who demonstrate poor compliance with treatment. These patients need to be hospitalized to ensure abstinence and titration of a proper lithium dose.

## ANTIDEPRESSANTS

Antidepressants do not directly alter substance abuse behavior but may be an important adjunct in the treatment of patients with primary depressive disorders. Determining the antidepressant of choice follows considerations of the depressive subtype and side-effect profile of the medications. Particular caution should be exercised in prescribing MAO inhibitors to alcoholics. Tyramine in wine products may precipitate a hypertensive crisis in conjunction with MAO use. Judgment, impulse control, and cognition may be impaired with alcoholics in early recovery. The risk of alcohol use in certain individuals may be unacceptable. In addition, intoxication may further impair judgment and increase the risk of using tyramine-containing products. Extreme caution should be used in placing alcoholics on MAO inhibitors when other antidepressants are counterindicated or inappropriate or when a clear case can be made for the use of MAO inhibitors as a first-line medication.

Gawin et al. reported successful use of desipramine in cocaine dependence (15). Desipramine in controlled double-blind studies has been shown to decrease craving and prevent relapse in primary cocaine addicts. Gawin et al. stress, however, the need for a comprehensive biopsychosocial approach to cocaine addiction that emphasizes cognitive behavioral approaches, manipulation of the individual's environment, life-style changes, and a more active interventional style on the part of the therapist. Desipramine is seen as an adjunct to the basic rehabilitation of the cocaine addict.

Desipramine is withheld for the first few days of abstinence to minimize the chance of cardiac arrhythmia. Desipramine is usually started at 50 mg and raised to 150 to 200 mg over a seven-day period. This regimen is maintained for three months and then discontinued. This approach is best indicated in chronic heavy intranasal or free-base use. Low- to moderate-level users respond adequately in most cases to nonpharmacologic treatment alone.

## BROMOCRIPTINE

Bromocriptine has been studied in the treatment of cocaine addiction. Cocaine has been hypothesized as producing neuronal dopamine depletion in certain parts of the brain with chronic use. Dopamine depletion also has a hypothesized association with cocaine craving. Recent evidence shows that cocaine may affect functioning of dopamine systems. Persistent evaluation of plasma prolactin levels after cocaine withdrawal has been reported and may reflect chronic inhibition of dopamine functioning. Bromocriptine may have some value in the acute onset of abstinence (first three to four days) by diminishing cocaine craving.

More studies are needed, however, to justify bromocriptine's general clinical use. Dosages range from 1.5 mg/day to 2.5 mg three times a day. Side effects may be dose related and include nausea, headache, and psychosis.

## CLONIDINE

Clonidine's use in detoxification has been discussed previously. Clonidine has also been reported to be helpful in alcohol withdrawal; these findings, however, are preliminary.

## PROPRANOLOL

The use of propranolol, a beta-one blocker, to control tremors and tachycardia in alcohol withdrawal is controversial and not routinely advocated.

## NEUROLEPTICS

As a rule, neuroleptics have no place in the treatment of primary alcoholism. They can lower seizure threshold and have the long-term risk of tardive dyskinesia. Neuroleptics can be very useful in psychosis across a wide spectrum of toxic drug reactions. They can be used adjunctively with benzodiazepines in the treatment of DTs. Neuroleptics are the primary treatment of choice in alcohol hallucinosis. Neuroleptics may also be useful during amphetamine-, cocaine-, PCP-, or marijuana-induced psychosis. In addition, neuroleptics may be indicated for the treatment of underlying psychiatric disorders.

## BENZODIAZEPINES

Benzodiazepines are the treatment of choice for alcohol or benzodiazepine detoxification. More dubious is the use of benzodiazepines in the rehabilitation outpatient setting. After clearance of withdrawal symptomatology, many patients still have a subacute withdrawal syndrome or the presence of an underlying anxiety disorder. An underlying anxiety disorder may be especially prevalent in high-dose benzodiazepine abusers, in agoraphobics, or in socially inept patients who may have panic or generalized anxiety disorders. Individuals who have had a clear history of anxiety disorder preceding alcohol or other CNS abuse may have a relapse of symptoms on detoxification. These patients pose a particularly difficult dilemma for the clinician. Often it is difficult to distinguish from underlying disorders, anxiety symptoms associated with chronic subacute withdrawal, reactive fear, and anxiety about withdrawal.

Additional difficulties arise with the presence of an underlying anxiety disorder. Benzodiazepines are very effective in suppressing anxiety symptoms and work through the gamma-aminobutyric acid (GABA) receptor. A recent work has outlined a combined benzodiazepine-GABA receptor system (16). Benzodiazepines also produce tolerance with psychological and physical dependence. Benzodiazepines are generally contraindicated in any psychoactive substance abuse disorder when not used for detoxification purposes. Whenever possible, more specific medication should be prescribed (e.g., desipramine or MAO inhibitors for panic attacks and a neuroleptic for psychotic disorders). Special problems exist in treating generalized anxiety disorders with secondary substance abuse. Effective utilization of other treatment modalities and setting firm limits on the use of psychoactive substances is needed. These patients often come to treatment after having used large doses of benzodiazepines. After detoxification, these patients may be extremely anxious and dysphoric, and temptations to relieve this suffering may lead clinicians to reinstate addictive substances. Despite appropriate treatment, these patients may have a poor outcome prognosis.

Benzodiazepines are also useful as an adjunct in treating acute agitation during PCP, lysergic acid diethylamide (LSD), or marijuana intoxication.

## BUSPIRONE

Buspirone (Buspar) is a new anxiolytic with no CNS depressant activity. Clinical studies have so far demonstrated little abuse potential or withdrawal syndrome. It apparently does not potentiate the effects of alcohol. Although theoretically buspirone would be a useful adjunct in the treatment of generalized anxiety or transient anxiety in substance abusers, there has not been enough clinical experience to justify this claim. Buspirone has the clinical disadvantage of having a slow onset of efficacy (up to three weeks); it is therefore of little use in transient anxiety disorders.

## METHADONE AND NALOXONE

The treatment of narcotic addiction has been described previously. Naloxone and other opioid antagonists may have some future use in other substance abuse disorders. Opioid-receptor functioning has been hypothesized to be associated with the etiology of alcohol dependence. In one preliminary study, naloxone has shown some benefit in recovering alcoholics.

**MISCELLANEOUS MEDICATIONS**

Potent serotonin reuptake inhibitors such as fluoxetine or zimelidine are being studied for their use in alcohol recovery. Chlormethiazole has shown promise in the treatment of alcohol detoxification in Europe but is not available in this country. The GABA agonist (i.e. calcium bisacetyl homotaurine) may have some potential use in preventing relapse in recovering alcoholics. A benzodiazepine antagonist, RO15-1788, has been found to antagonize the action of alcohol at the receptor level. Clinical implications are not yet clear for this drug, which may help reverse some effects of overdose. It may not help reduce other toxic effects and is likely to play a limited clinical role. Amantadine has been reported to be useful in the short-term cessation of cocaine craving.

## FAMILY EVALUATION AND THERAPY

Every patient with addictions should have a thorough diagnostic evaluation of the family; information from family members may be crucial both in making the diagnosis and in consideration of treatment planning (17). Family treatment is frequently indicated, especially in those families in which considerable support is available to the patient. The children of alcoholics may especially benefit from family evaluation and treatment. Frequently, family members have been affected in major ways by the patient's problems. Frequently, the family system has been altered to accommodate the patient's drinking and may to some degree reinforce it. Confrontation by family members in many cases provides the stimulus to the patient's initially seeking treatment and may be important in helping the patient remain in treatment. Family treatments based on the concept of "the alcoholic system" focus on the correction of dysfunctional patterns of interactional behavior within the family and measure success not only by achieving abstinence but also by improving the level of functioning in the family.

Techniques employed by family therapists include conjoint family therapy, marital therapy groups, and conjoint hospitalization for marital couples. Galanter et al. emphasized the network approach of involving family or friends to provide necessary support for the patient between the initial sessions (18). Contacts between network members include telephone calls, dinner arrangements, and social encounters and are planned during joint sessions.

## SELF-HELP

Every clinician needs to be thoroughly familiar with the work of the Twelve-Step self-help programs: AA, Alanon, NA, Substance Anonymous, Cocaine Anonymous, Gamblers Anonymous, and Overeaters Anonymous. In addition to an understanding of Twelve-Step approaches to addictive disorders, every clinician should have the personal experience of having attended meetings of both AA and Alanon to be in touch with what patients experience while attending these meetings.

AA was formed in 1935 by Bill Wilson and Dr. Robert Smith in Akron, Ohio, in part due to lack of available medical treatment for alcoholism. It had its roots in the Oxford movement, which later became the moral rearmament movement; after a slow start, it has grown into a far-flung, huge international grass roots network that includes more than 2 million members and 185,000 groups worldwide. The major message of the organization is that people with addictive problems, through recognition of alcoholism as an illness, can achieve sobriety together through a spiritual program that includes accepting powerlessness over alcohol and dependency on some intervention beyond the self. It is a voluntary self-supporting fellowship that avoids any self-serving political or economic activity.

### HOW IT WORKS

The Twelve-Step program involves a series of steps and traditions that rely heavily on self-honesty, sobriety, group process, humility, provision of successful role models, self-care, and destigmatization of alcoholism as an illness. In Alanon, family members have a parallel program that includes self-help for the family and has grown to 26,000 groups. Other family-oriented programs that are rapidly growing include Alateen, for teenage users and teenage children of alcoholics, and a movement of groups for adult children of alcoholics. Although the Twelve-Step program is frequently recommended in conjunction with a variety of other treatment approaches, for many patients the program may suffice as the sole treatment for alcoholism and other drug problems. On average, members attend approximately four meetings per week, although in the early stages many attend 90 meetings in 90 days. Multiply-addicted patients may attend several different Twelve-Step programs. A variety of categories of meetings include open meetings that the interested public may attend, closed meetings, beginners meetings, discussion groups, and homogeneous groups. Although meetings vary in style, there is generally a warm, family feel and a sense of acceptance and understanding that permeates most groups. The assumption is that alcoholics intuitively understand and can identify with universal problems faced by other alcoholics and can share feelings in a group. An emphasis on self-help through helping others with the same problem has contributed widely to the success of this group, and a large part of the spirituality of the program is embedded in the generosity in time and energy of its members. A system of sponsorship of members by experienced AA goers and the development of a support network of exchanged telephone numbers are other important elements of its membership. AA provides an opportunity for people to practice relatedness, gain structure, test values, test judgment, practice honesty, find acceptance, and regain hope (19).

## THE ILLNESS MODEL

Throughout history an illness model of alcoholism has at one or another time surfaced, often in parallel with strongly held moralistic views of alcoholism. In his design of the Twelve Steps, Bill Wilson helped destigmatize alcoholism. In 1954, the American Medical Association officially supported the disease concept, which is endorsed by the American Psychiatric Association. Another contribution of the self-help movement has been an understanding that alcoholism and drug abuse can be primary disorders and that treatment of other disorders is not possible without also addressing this primary disorder.

## NEW DEVELOPMENTS IN AA

Although AA began with treatment solely of patients with

alcoholism and originally was primarily an organization of white middle-class men with severe alcoholism, recent years have seen many people get help earlier in the course of their illness, and there has been a dramatic increase in the number of women who attend AA meetings. An expansion into the younger population, with more dual addiction and with additional psychiatric problems, has led to greater attention to subpopulations with particular needs of their own. Homogeneous subgroups have developed, such as gay AA groups, physician AA groups, groups of adult children of alcoholics, atheist and agnostic AA groups, AA groups for human immunodeficiency virus (HIV) positive patients, and AA groups for patients with dual diagnosis.

## REFERRALS TO TWELVE-STEP PROGRAMS

The therapist may take an active role in referring to AA in addition to monitoring and interpreting resistances to regular attendance. The physician can either have the patient call AA directly from the physician's office or may call for the patient in order to select a meeting for the patient to attend. A phone listing for AA intergroup is easily obtainable, and volunteers are very helpful at providing information about meetings suited to the individual patient.

Clinicians may help reduce concerns or negative responses that may be felt by patients on their first AA meetings. Initially, patients may have difficulties understanding AA policies and may question aspects of the AA program. Patients who have negative reactions to the spiritual aspects of the AA program or who feel criticized in AA because of use of psychiatric medications or not accepted because of polysubstance abuse will need explanation and support. Patients should be encouraged to get an AA sponsor.

## ACTIVITY THERAPY

Inpatient rehabilitation programs and many organized day and evening hospital programs offer occupational and recreational therapy. Because patients have often had difficulties both in finding and holding on to jobs, employment-related counseling may be very useful. This may include assessing skills and determining suitability for various forms of employment, outplacement, and helping the patient deal with job-related problems that may have resulted from addiction. For patients whose workaholism contributed to alcoholism, recreational therapy may be helpful in teaching relaxation techniques and improved utilization of unstructured time. Some workaholic patients have rewarded themselves with use of substances rather than finding other ways of tension release and enjoyment. Interest in exercise, hobbies, and the arts may provide an important substitution for substances as a means of tension release (20).

## COUNSELING

Certified alcohol and drug counselors have increasingly played prominent roles in alcohol and drug treatment programs. Counselors are involved in every phase of treatment, including evaluation, psychoeducation, individual and group counseling, and aftercare. In the area of relapse prevention, counselors frequently provide support, advice, and valuable information regarding treatment, including information about the Twelve-Step program.

## EDUCATION

Most treatment programs include active education about alcohol and drug effects, the addictive process, complications, effects on the family, treatment alternatives, Twelve-Step self-help programs, and relapse prevention. Education helps reduce fear, guilt, and shame; supports the medical model; and provides hope. Use of lectures, discussion groups, films, books, and homework assignments are an important part of the work of treatment and help keep patients productively engaged during treatment.

## ■ TREATMENT OF MENTALLY ILL, CHEMICALLY ABUSING PATIENTS

The most commonly seen psychiatric patients have more than one psychiatric diagnosis, and the most frequent accompanying diagnoses are psychoactive substance use disorders. The diagnostic, treatment, and etiologic implications of the interactions between substance use disorders and other psychiatric diagnoses must be taken into account in treatment planning. Interactions of substance use disorders with affective disorders, anxiety disorders, organic disorders, personality disorders, schizophrenia, anorexia nervosa, and sexual orientation disorders are common.

Psychoactive substance use disorders can mask, mimic, or result from a wide variety of psychiatric and medical disorders. The role of the psychiatrist is to provide a sophisticated understanding of substance use disorders in relation to other psychiatric illness and to determine the course of action at the most appropriate level, be it psychosocial or medical. Every patient with substance abuse problems needs a careful psychiatric assessment and treatment plan. Conversely, a thorough substance use history is an essential part of all psychiatric interviews.

Longitudinal, adoption, epidemiologic, and family studies have not finally settled old questions as to the cause, effect, or coexistent relationship between psychopathology and addictive behavior (21). Most studies support the idea that the inherited predisposition to an addictive problem is independent of other psychiatric disorders. The trait of addiction may be primary to psychiatric illness, may develop as a way of coping with other problems, or may coexist with other psychiatric disorders. Treatment planning for MICA patients depends on flexibility and a broad understanding of psychiatry as well as of alcohol and drug abuse.

## THE CHALLENGING PATIENT WITH DUAL DIAGNOSIS

Complex interactions between psychopathology and addictions are hard to separate clinically because of overlapping signs and symptoms resulting from intoxication, withdrawal, mixed drug reactions, adverse drug responses, medical conditions, and the organic and psychosocial effects of substance use on affective state, anxiety, or personality. The addition of other Axis I, II, and III disorders (22) complicates diagnoses and makes treatment more difficult.

Estimates are that 20 to 50 percent of the psychiatric treatment population also abuse substances. The need to treat simultaneously two disorders, with different treatment needs, has strained the mental health system. The medical community, the government, and society in general have been slow to respond to the treatment needs of patients that generate such therapeutic pessimism. The system has been caught short of personnel who are trained to address the treatment of psychiatric disorders and substance abuse adequately. Personnel in the mental health field and the substance abuse field should have the rudimentary knowledge to screen patients properly and to develop a treatment plan that adequately addresses the patient's needs. Several model programs have been developed around the country to integrate psychiatric and substance abuse treatment. These special programs are not readily available at this point, and the dual-diagnosis patient often falls through the cracks of the treatment system. Severe psychiatric disorders often preclude full treatment in substance abuse clinics or self-help groups. Confrontational techniques and self-exposure, done in some substance abuse programs, may exacerbate psychiatric symptoms. Special AA and NA groups are being formed for dual-diagnosis or "double trouble" patients. Discussions around the role of medications should be addressed. The work of McLellan, Woody, and O'Brien has had important treatment implications. High psychiatric severity patients benefit significantly by additional professional psychiatric therapy (23). Some patients, especially patients with frank psychosis or suicidal ideation, require primary psychiatric settings (e.g., day hospital or inpatient setting). This should not preclude, however, addressing substance abuse issues. Attendance at AA or NA meetings should be arranged if possible. A substance abuse specialist should be available to psychiatric facilities with a high number of dual-diagnosis patients. The substance abuse specialist may be best used as part of a multidisciplinary team approach.

A discussion of treatment of dual-diagnosis patients would not be complete without the recognition of some of the pressing social needs of these patients. Often these patients have alienated family, friends, and treatment personnel. The need for adequate housing, health, and follow-up is imperative. Residential facilities are needed to ease the transition of these patients into society. Coordination of the various agencies is needed. Talbott discussed the case management approach extensively (24). Often substance abuse facilities refuse admission to psychiatric patients, and psychiatric halfway houses refuse admission to patients with a history of substance abuse.

# ■ TREATMENT OUTCOME STUDIES

## *PROBLEMS IN METHODOLOGY*

In comparing research on the treatment outcome of addictive disorders, the following factors can affect outcome: the demographics; severity of illness of patients selected; inadequate controls; other specific treatments inside of, outside of, and after the clearly defined test treatment; data analysis; duration of follow-up; and a variety of other problems including the possibility of researcher bias. Although most studies indicate positive results for alcoholism treatment, the differential therapeutics of modality, setting, and therapist's characteristics have been hard to demonstrate. The question of which treatments are best for which patients remains the problem in the substance abuse area as well as for the rest of psychiatry.

Tie scores have been found in using different treatment modalities or lengths of stays, especially when the intensity of treatment has been low in both experimental and control groups. Edwards, comparing patients who received only advice versus patients getting "intensive" outpatient treatment, found poor results for both treatment groups, possibly related in part to a lack of therapeutic zeal on the part of the researchers (25). In other less well-controlled studies by highly motivated clinicians using more intense treatments with a more upper-middle-class population, favorable results have been reported using their preferred modes of treatment (26).

## *PATIENT CHARACTERISTICS*

Positive treatment outcome is most frequently found in patients who have high socioeconomic stability, low antisocial personality, a lack of psychiatric and medical problems, and a negative family history for alcoholism. History of contact with AA, positive work history, stable marriage, high social class, and fewer arrests are correlated with better outcome. The Hazelden Treatment Center reported success rates as high as 62 percent after 18 months, with a follow-up response rate of 75 percent (27). Gordis et al. found a 32 percent success rate in a program that served an inner-city population with high unemployment (28). Although most studies of treatment settings have not differentiated outcome based on setting, a problem in these studies has been that patients were often not randomly assigned to an inpatient setting. Sicker patients are more often hospitalized and are likely to stay for longer treatments.

## MATCHING TREATMENTS TO PATIENTS

In a study of Welte et al., patients who stayed in the hospital longer were more likely to be abstaining or drinking less at follow-up (29). Bromet and Moos found that longer-stay patients had reduced relapse rates (30). In a series of classic studies, McLellan et al. found that severity of psychiatric disturbance correlates with treatment outcome for psychoactive substance use disorder and also predicts which kind of treatment settings may be needed for psychiatrically ill patients (31). Patients with high severity of psychiatric problems did poorly regardless of modality or treatment setting. Patients who had legal problems did poorly in inpatient programs. Patients with the least severe psychiatric problems did well in inpatient and outpatient settings. It was those patients in the middle range of severity of psychiatric problems who also had employment or family problems, needed inpatient care, and did better when psychiatric services were also provided.

McLellan et al.'s work found an overall good effectiveness for alcohol treatment; that treatment is improved when patients are matched to appropriate setting (32). Outcome measures include decrement in drinking and family problems, reduction of severity of psychiatric problems, and increases in income. The Philadelphia group found that appropriate treatment of psychiatric diagnoses concomitant with substance use disorders improves treatment outcome for other poor-prognosis patients. Alcohol treatment programs have been found to be cost effective and to reduce inpatient and outpatient medical costs.

## GOALS OF TREATMENT

In a large outcome study by Heltzer et al. over five to seven years, only 1.6 percent of patients were found to be drinking moderately, which indicates that stable moderate drinking is likely to be a rare outcome among treated alcoholics (33). In 1982, following 61 hospitalized alcoholics in a four-year study, Petinatti found a return to normal Minnesota Multiphasic Personality Inventory (MMPI) profiles in subjects who maintained long-term abstinence and found no hospitalization for those who achieved complete abstinence (34). These studies emphasize the importance of abstinence as the best goal for alcoholic patients and the problems in predicting which patients are likely to be the rare ones to return to nonproblem drinking in a follow-up period (35).

## ■ RELAPSE

What is relapse? Is relapse a return to the preabstinence level of alcohol or drug use? Is it any use of alcohol or drugs? Is it a loss of resolution toward changing some alcohol or substance abuse behavior? Is relapse only the active resuming of drug or alcohol abuse or can certain behaviors be labeled on a continuum in the process of relapse? Does the substitution of another form of addictive behavior (e.g., overeating, overworking, or gambling) constitute a relapse? Can relapse be identified only after a determined resolution to stop alcohol or drugs?

Relapse can best be described as a process of attitudinal change that usually results in reuse of alcohol or drugs. Relapse is an important clinical phenomenon in the natural course of alcohol or substance abuse. In fact, addictions can be described as diseases with the characteristic of recurrent relapses. Estimates are that more than 90 percent of patients in any one 12-month period after initiating a period of abstinence will use psychoactive substances; 45 to 50 percent will return to pretreatment levels of morbidity (36). Thus it is extremely important that patients who have committed themselves to the recovery process understand and anticipate the possibility of relapse. They need to develop coping strategies and contingency plans to thwart the onset of relapse, minimize the extent of damage, and promote renewed abstinence quickly.

## RELAPSE PREVENTION

There has been a keen interest in relapse prevention in recent years. Many of the cognitive behavioral techniques of general psychology are being applied successfully to the addictions. The general principle behind many of these techniques is to have the patient involved in understanding his or her own unique set of high-risk relapse situations and in employing alternative coping techniques. Prior to relapse prevention training, what is stressed is a thorough understanding of one's own self-motivational reasons for discontinuing addictive behavior and being able to work through alternative responses to situations and choosing abstinence as part of the best mode of response.

## HIGH-RISK SITUATIONS

In relapse prevention, identification of early signs of stress and attitudinal changes or coping mechanisms are employed. High-risk situations are identified. Marlatt and Gordon identified eight categories of high-risk drinking situations that could be applicable to other substance abuse: unpleasant emotions, physical discomfort, pleasant emotions, testing personal control, urges and temptations, conflict with others, social pressure to drink, and pleasant times with others (37). The strength of any one situation being the highest risk can vary among individuals or drug classes. For example, young early abusers may be more susceptible to use during positive feelings. Older, more chronic users may relapse more often due to depression or guilt. Abuse of opiates and cocaine may be more heavily tied to environmental cues. For example, a cocaine addict has a harder time saying no if drugs are offered than an alcoholic who is offered a drink. Adolescents may be more susceptible to peer pressure.

It is important to identify and watch for thoughts and feelings that typically occur during these high-risk situations. Several rating scales are being developed to rate high-risk situations systematically. Homework assignments, complete with relapse prevention workbooks, teach patients the ins and outs of the relapse process, help them develop alternative coping skills, and reinforce the experience of a sense of self-mastery in these situations. Relapse prevention is especially valuable in outpatient settings, where opportunities are present to practice skills in a natural environment. Behavioral techniques such as role playing and assertiveness training are also valuable.

## GUILT AND SHAME REDUCTION

The result of this work may allow a patient to see relapse not as an "all-or-none" phenomenon and not as an unforeseeable or unavoidable event. Relapse defined as a change in one's resolution to change is a fairly common experience that all of us have at times. Relapse in this sense is a fact of everyday life. Understanding this may prevent the feeling that the patient has totally failed if a return to drug use occurs and negates the feeling that all is lost. Marlatt and Gordon coined the term *abstinence violation effect* to describe this attitude, which implies that once drug use occurs, it must inevitably lead to pretreatment level of use (37). Guilt, shame, a sense of lack of control, trapped feelings, and a lack of prespecified plan may escalate drug use. The immediate benefit of drug use may overshadow the realization of the negative long-term consequences.

## PRACTICING SOCIAL SKILLS

Identifying patients' personal strengths, past coping behaviors, and environmental supports is important. Examples of alternative coping mechanisms when faced with temptation or drug use include calling a friend or sponsor, leaving the setting, or refusing the next drink. Relapse prevention may require, especially in the early stages of recovery, avoidance of high-risk situations and cues. Later on in the process, some avoidable high-risk situations can be mastered with alternative coping skills. Social skills training has also been used in prevention. In some situations, however, it may be advisable to avoid cues at all cost (e.g., having a "crack" addict not return to a setting where cocaine is being used).

## ACHIEVING RECOVERY

The concept of abstinence is different from the concept of recovery or sobriety. Recovery implies the process in which the individual is not only not using drugs, but developing a normal, balanced life-style, healthy self-esteem, and healthy intimacy in a sense of meaningful living. For addictive patients, recovery is a never-ending process; the term *cure* is avoided.

## ■ REFERENCES

1. Frances A, Clarkin J, Perry S: Differential Therapeutics in Psychiatry. New York, Brunner/Mazel, 1984
2. Allen M, Frances R: Alcoholism and other psychopathology, in Psychopathology and Addictive Disorders. Edited by Meyer RE. New York, Guilford Press, 1986
3. Mirin SM, Weiss RD, Sollogub A, et al: Affective illness in substance abusers, in Substance Abuse and Psychopathology. Washington, DC, American Psychiatric Press, 1984, pp 58–77
4. Nicholson DP: The immediate management of overdose. Med Clin North Am 1983; 67:1279–1293
5. Dreisbach RH: Handbook of Poisoning, 11th ed. Los Altos, CA, Lange Medical Publishers, 1983
6. Goldberg MJ, Spector R, Park GD, et al: An approach to the management of the poisoned patient. Arch Intern Med 1986; 146:1381–1385
7. Park GD, Spector R, Goldberg MJ, et al: Expanded role of charcoal therapy in the poisoned and overdosed patient. Arch Intern Med 1986; 146:669–673
8. Moskowitz G, Chalmers TC, Sacks HS, et al: Deficiencies of clinical trials of alcohol withdrawal. Alcoholism: Clinical and Experimental Research 1983; Winter, 41–46
9. Frances RJ, Franklin JE: Alcohol-induced organic mental disorders, in The American Psychiatric Press Textbook of Neuropsychiatry. Edited by Hales RE, Yudofsky SC. Washington, DC, American Psychiatric Press, 1987
10. Frances RJ, Alexopoulos GS: The inpatient treatment of the alcoholic patient. Psychiatric Annals 1982; 12:386–391
11. Frances RJ, Khantzian EJ, Tamerin JS: Psychodynamic psychotherapy, in Treatments of Psychiatric Disorders: A Task Force Report of the American Psychiatric Association. Washington, DC, American Psychiatric Association, 1989

12. Kaufman MD, Reoux J: Guidelines for the successful psychotherapy of substance abusers. Am J Drug Alcohol Abuse 1988; 14:199–209

13. Cooper DE: The role of group psychotherapy in the treatment of substance abuse. Am J Psychother 1987; 41:55–61

14. Fawcett J, Clark DC, Aagesen CA, et al: A double-blind, placebo-controlled trial of lithium carbonate therapy for alcoholism. Arch Gen Psychiatry 1987; 44:248–256

15. Gawin FH, Kleber HD, et al: Desipramine facilitation of initial cocaine abstinence. Arch Gen Psychiatry 46:117–121, 1989

16. Skolnick P, Paul SM: Benzodiazepine receptors in the central nervous system. Int Rev Neurobiol 23:103–140, 1982

17. Steinglass P: Experimenting with family treatment approaches to alcoholism, 1950–1975: a review. Fam Process 1976; 15:97–123

18. Galanter M, Castaneda R, Salamon I: Institutional self-help therapy for alcoholism: clinical outcome. Alcoholism: Clinical and Experimental Research 1987; 11:424–429

19. Emrick CD: Alcoholics Anonymous: affiliation processes and effectiveness as treatment. Alcoholism: Clinical and Experimental Research 1987; 11:416–423

20. Gorski T, Miller M: Learning to Live Again: Guidelines for Recovery. Kansas, Human Ecology Systems, 1982

21. Schuckit MA: Genetic and clinical implications of alcoholism and affective disorder. Am J Psychiatry 1986; 143:140–147

22. American Psychiatric Association: Diagnostic and Statistical Manual of Mental Disorders, 3rd ed, revised. Washington, DC, American Psychiatric Association, 1987

23. Woody GE, McLellan T, Luboruky L, et al: Severity of psychiatric symptoms as a predictor of benefits from psychotherapy: The Veterans Administration Penn Study. Am J Psychiatry 141:1172–1177, 1985

24. Talbott J (ed): The Chronic Mentally Ill: Treatment, Programs, Systems. New York, Human Sciences Press, 1981

25. Edwards G, Orford J, Egert S, et al: Alcoholism: a controlled trial of "treatment" and "advice." Journal of Studies on Alcohol 38:1004–1031, 1977

26. Ornstein P, Cherepon JA: Demographic variables as predictors of alcoholism treatment outcome. J Stud Alcohol 1985; 46:425–432

27. Patton M: Validity and reliability of Hazelden treatment follow-up data. City Center, MN, Hazelden Educational Services, 1979

28. Gordis E, Dorph D, Sepe V, et al: Outcome of alcoholism treatment among 5,578 patients in an urban comprehensive hospital-based program: application of a computerized data system. Alcoholism: Clinical and Experimental Research 1981; 5:509–522

29. Welte J, Hynes G, Sokolow L, et al: Effect of length of stay in

inpatient alcoholism treatment on outcome. J Stud Alcohol 1981; 42:483–491

30. Bromet E, Moos RH: Environmental resources and the posttreatment functioning of alcoholic patients. J Health Soc Behav 1977; 18:326–338

31. McLellan AT, Luborsky L, Woody GE, et al: Predicting response to drug and alcohol treatments: Role of psychiatric severity. Arch Gen Psychiatry 1983, 40:620–625

32. McLellan AT, Druley KA, O'Brien CP, et al: Matching substance abuse patients to appropriate treatments: The Addiction Severity Index. Drug Alcohol Depend 1980; 5:189–195

33. Helzer JE, Robins LN, Taylor JR, et al: The extent of long-term moderate drinking among alcoholics discharged from medical and psychiatric treatment facilities. N Eng J Med 1985; 312:1678–1682

34. Pettinati HW, Sugarman A, Maurer HS: Four year MMPI changes in abstinent and drinking alcoholics. Alcoholism: Clinical and Experimental Research 6:487–494, 1982

35. Wanberg KW, Horn JL: Alcoholism symptom patterns of men and women: a comparative study. Quarterly Journal of Studies on Alcohol, 1970; 31:40–61

36. Armour D, Polich J, Stambul H: Alcoholism and Treatment. New York, John Wiley & Sons, 1978

37. Marlatt G, Gordon J: Relapse Prevention. New York, Guilford Press, 1985

# 9 TREATMENT APPROACHES TO SPECIFIC POPULATIONS

## ■ WOMEN

Although there have been increasing trends for more women to be in treatment, there probably has been no major increase in alcoholism among women in the United States (1). More women have sought treatment, and the stigma associated with being a female alcoholic has decreased. However, women remain underrepresented in alcohol treatment programs, and their special needs in treatment programs are not always addressed. Male alcoholics outnumber females by 2 to 1; however, there are three to four times as many men in treatment as women. With increasing numbers of women in the workplace, greater numbers are being identified by the employee assistance programs (EAPs). More frequently, men are being caught for drinking and driving and are likely to be arrested for public intoxication and referred to treatment programs as a result. The possibility of fetal alcohol syndrome contributes greater urgency to identification of female alcoholism and intravenous (iv) drug use to reduce fetal effects of drugs and human immunodeficiency virus (HIV) transmission in iv addicts. More frequently, women present with coexisting depression compared to men and less frequently have accompanying antisocial problems. Frequently, women have had sexual abuse in childhood and alcoholism and drug abuse as an adult. Alcoholism and drug abuse in women may also be associated with panic and anxiety disorders.

## GENETICS, CULTURAL, AND BIOLOGIC EFFECTS

Most research on the heredity of alcoholism has been done on men. Recent studies indicate a genetic potential for alcoholism in women as well, however, although it may very well be that this is frequently overridden by culture. Alcoholism in women varies markedly, depending on culture. The female to male ratio for Americans is 1 to 2; for Koreans it is 1 to 28. Women have a higher blood alcohol level (BAL) pound per pound compared with men and have changing BAL effects at different times in the menstrual cycle. Women are most frequently admitted to alcohol treatment hospitals during the peri-menstrual time, which is often marked by heavier drinking. In addition to lower tolerance for alcohol, women tend to have more telescoped course of the chronic effects of excessive drinking, including cirrhosis of the liver, compared with men. Alcohol and drugs in women may sometimes be used to reduce sexual inhibitions. Although ultimately alcohol may reduce desire and ability to perform sexually in women as in men, initially it may be disinhibiting.

## TREATMENT ISSUES

Women in traditional treatment programs often experience discomfort when talking about sexual abuse and sexual issues in mixed male-female groups. Women may feel intimidated and outnumbered by men in alcohol rehabilitation programs. For this reason, women's groups in rehabilitation programs are beneficial. In general, treatment for alcoholism and drug abuse in women is similar to treatment for men. Important special treatment considerations include watching especially closely for the possibility of sedative-hypnotic dependence, anxiety disorders and depression, extrasensitivity to stigma, and awareness of fetal alcohol and drug effects. Meeting recovered alcoholic women role models and working with female professionals may also be a factor in improved self-esteem.

Secondary alcoholism with self-medication for anxiety, panic, or depression is a much more frequent finding in women compared with men. Sometimes alcoholism may develop after benzodiazepine dependence, which may have started from efforts at treating anxiety disorders. Careful use of medication in women of childbearing age includes awareness of relative risks and benefits. Treatment of depression and anxiety disorders in women with dual diagnosis is often necessary. Inpatient treatment poses special problems for young mothers, and few programs exist in which women can be hospitalized along with their children. There are also increased fears of loss of custody in alcoholic women and increased needs for child-care services. Women frequently have economic problems that may make it more difficult for them to get good treatment.

## ACQUIRED IMMUNE DEFICIENCY SYNDROME (AIDS)

Fifty-thousand women are AIDS positive in New York; the principal route of spread in women relates to drugs both in terms of HIV use and in being a sexual partner of an HIV user (2). Five hundred babies have been born who are HIV positive, and one in 25 babies in the Newark, New Jersey, area is born HIV positive. Minority women are especially at high risk. Two-thirds of women in methadone programs in the Bronx, New York, are HIV positive and two-thirds of these are mothers. Prostitution in women can be another cause of AIDS spread and is also frequently associated with HIV drug use. There is likely to be an increasingly greater impact on women in the future as the risk pool expands to include partners of HIV users and possibly heterosexuals.

A special concern of women is the possibility of contracting AIDS through intercourse with men who are iv drug users. Women who use substances may frequently take more risks, have poorer self-care, and less frequently insist on use of condoms and on refusal of unsafe sexual practices with their iv-using partners. Women who are iv users of childbearing age are at special high risk and need careful counseling.

## FETAL ALCOHOL SYNDROME

Fetal alcohol syndrome occurs in approximately one in 1,000 live births generally and as high as one in 100 births in some Eskimo villages. Typical signs of fetal alcohol syndrome include low birth rate, growth deficiency with delayed motor development, mental retardation and learning problems, and other less severe fetal alcohol behavioral effects. No safe alcohol level has been established, and dangers increase with dose used.

## ■ CHILDREN AND ADOLESCENTS

The use, abuse, and treatment of psychoactive substances in children and adolescents has been a major focus of attention for parents, school personnel, law enforcement agencies, and mental health professionals. Substance abuse can interfere with natural growth and normal interaction and development, including relationships with peers, performance in school, attitudes toward law and authority, and acute and chronic organic effects. The question of when use becomes abuse and dependency in adolescents is problematic. There is a continuum between hazardous, harmful use and abuse. It is more difficult to diagnose dependence in adolescents because of the reduced likelihood of signs and symptoms of withdrawal that frequently occur later in addiction. Adolescents are less likely to report withdrawal symptoms, have shorter periods of addiction, and may recover more rapidly from withdrawal symptoms. Early identification of patterns of drug use that interfere with relationships, school performance, and ability to provide good self-care are important in addition to physiologic symptoms of tolerance and withdrawal (3).

## EXTENT OF THE PROBLEM

In 1985, a Michigan high school survey found that 65 percent of 12- to 17-year-olds had used alcohol; 27 percent had used marijuana; 7 percent had used stimulants; 2 percent had used phencyclidine (PCP); 5 percent had used lysergic acid diethylamide (LSD); and less than 5 percent had tried heroin (4). A 1987 survey of high school seniors found that 23 percent used marijuana (4 percent used it daily); 5.5 percent used amphetamines; and 4.1 percent used crack. Six out of 10 high school graduates have tried at least one illicit drug at least once (5). Although there have been some recent declines in the use of marijuana, the frequency of cocaine has increased since 1983. Greater availability of cocaine, lower price, and new forms of administration (e.g., smoking "crack") have led to higher use and greater dependence on cocaine. A recent decline in drugs, with the exception of cocaine, may partly be the result of increased mass media coverage of negative aspects of addictive behavior, combined with school-based programs and increased attention to health promotion and fitness.

## CONTRIBUTING FACTORS

Peer group, school environment, age, geography, race, values, family attitudes toward substance abuse, and biologic predisposition are all contributing factors to adolescent substance abuse. Nonuser adolescents are more likely to describe close relationships with their parents than users. They are more likely to be comfortably dependent on their parents and closer to family than users, who report themselves as independent and distant. Users more frequently indicate that they do not want to be like their parents and do not feel they need their approval; they did not acknowledge a desire for affection from their parents. Frequently, there is a positive family history for chemical dependence in adolescents with substance abuse problems. Genetic studies indicate a strong hereditary predisposition to alcoholism.

## FAMILIES

Families play a more important role among adolescents compared to adult substance abusers and are a more important part of treatment. Parents and family members of adolescent abusers are less resistant to being involved in treatment because the adolescent usually resides with them and the parents may feel responsible for their behavior. Adolescents are less likely to enter treatment to avoid incarceration than adults, and are likely to be pushed into treatment by their families, by schools, and by pediatricians and family physicians.

## RESIDENTIAL TREATMENT

Inpatient or residential treatment for adolescents is indicated for those who have had a drug problem that has interfered with their ability to function in school, work, and home environments, and who have been unable to maintain abstinence through outpatient treatment. Low motivation for change, disruptive home life, high acting out, involvement with the juvenile justice system, and additional psychiatric or medical problems may all be additional reasons for inpatient treatment. Depression, suicidality, hyperactivity, chemical dependence, and overdoses of drugs are additional indications. Lengths of stays for adolescents tend to be longer than for adults. Langley Porter found a mean length of hospital stay of 132 days; mean length of stay in a study of therapeutic communities was 96 days (6). Adolescents frequently require longer hospital stays than adults because of greater dispositional problems, more resistance to treatment, greater difficulty of controlling acting out in outpatient therapy, and greater severity of family problems. Treatment outcome for adolescents is worse than for adults.

## DRUG INTOXICATION OR PSYCHOSIS

Drug-induced psychoses may last for a short period of time and are helped by providing a highly structured, quiet, supportive environment. Often it is not necessary to use medications unless the patient becomes agitated. Then benzodiazepines or, depending on severity of psychosis, antipsychotic medications are useful.

Intoxication with drugs and alcohol in adolescents may lead to disinhibition and violence. Strategies for managing these crises include a quiet, supportive environment that can lessen the chance of the child or adolescent acting out in a violent manner. Support staff may be needed to approach potentially violent adolescents and have an additional quieting effect (3). Police should be involved if the adolescent is carrying a weapon unless the situation is emergent and contains life-threatening circumstances. Emergency-room checks for weapons are very important with adolescents. Avoidance of use of minor tranquilizers with adolescent abusers is important in that benzodiazepines lead to increased disinhibition and increase the possibility of violent acting out.

## MENTALLY ILL, CHEMICALLY ABUSING ADOLESCENTS

Most adolescents entering inpatient drug and alcohol treatment programs have additional mental health problems, which include conduct disorder, affective disorder, anxiety disorders, and eating disorders, and other Axis I conditions as well as frequent Axis II diagnosis of passive-aggressive personality, borderline personality disorder, and narcissistic personality disorder (7).

Suicidal ideation and behavior is important with this population, and careful history taking regarding suicide attempts and thoughts is crucial. If there is a positive family history of suicide or depression, psychosis, isolation from families and friends, previous suicide attempts, clear-cut plans of suicide attempts, or violent means of carrying out the plan, the risk of suicide is increased. Substance abuse disorders are major risk factors for suicide among adolescents. Alcohol-related motor vehicle accidents are the leading cause of death among youth aged 15 to 24. There have also been a rash of recent reports of respiratory depression, coma, and death after excessive bouts of alcohol.

Increased alcohol and drug abuse in adolescents is frequently associated with risk-taking behavior linked to spread of HIV infection (e.g., iv drug use, unsafe sexual practices, and increased sexual activity with multiple partners). Substance use disorders in adolescents may also directly affect the immune system and, through stress, have indirect effects on the immune system. Sexual abuse of children and adolescents and families with substance abuse is not uncommon and may also increase risk of HIV spread to adolescents in families where an HIV user is present.

## ASSESSMENT

Assessment of the adolescent drug user requires a careful history of both patient and family, including where and when drugs are used, under what circumstances, dosages used, and what drug effects and reactions have occurred. Parents should be asked about the adolescent's behavior, personality changes, school performance and absenteeism, change in peers, presence of rebelliousness, and number of occasions they thought their adolescent was intoxicated. Parental drug use history is also important. Parents' reactions to the adolescent's drug use, whether confrontation has been tried, and the adolescent's previous response to confrontation are important. Gathering histories from schools, pediatricians, clergy, and probation officers is also useful. The clinician should be aware of the possibility of denial by the adolescent or family.

## CLINICAL MANAGEMENT ISSUES

The treatment of adolescents requires both structure and flexibility. Awareness of the possibility of contraband stashes and the necessity for intermittent urine screening are important in inpatient treatment programs to monitor compliance. Most programs rely heavily on a therapeutic milieu with individualized treatment planning. A warm, supportive environment with organized structure increases motivation and maximizes positive interaction with the peer group. Adolescent programs rely heavily on peer-support groups, family therapy, school, education on drug abuse, and Twelve-Step programs such as Alcoholics Anonymous (AA) and Alateen vocational programs, patient-staff meetings, and activity therapy. Programs that do best with adolescents encourage openness and spontaneous expression of feelings, allow patients to engage in independent decision making, have counselors help patients solve their real problems, use cognitive and behavioral approaches and relaxation techniques, have experienced counselors and staff, and frequently employ the support of volunteers.

## *RELAPSES*

Relapse prevention with adolescents is often more difficult than with adults and it becomes more difficult to achieve the goal of total abstinence. Rules such as "one drug use and you're out" are less likely to be effective on adolescent treatment services, where the adolescent may be looking for a means of escaping treatment. With adolescents, a slip needs to be understood as a symptom of the problem; the patient should not be rejected because of a relapse. Relapses may lead to adjustment of treatment plans and may require rehospitalization. Discharge planning needs to include outpatient treatment for drug abuse and frequent attendance at self-help support groups. Frequently, family or group treatments are added to individual treatment, depending on need. Urine screens for drug and alcohol are frequently part of a comprehensive outpatient plan. Adolescents may also need halfway houses, residential treatment centers, and in some instances long-term inpatient psychiatric care.

## ■ THE ELDERLY

The true scope of alcohol and drug abuse problems in the geriatric population is unknown. The incidence of alcoholism is lower in the elderly population. A greater and more frequent problem is overuse of prescription drugs and interaction of alcohol and other medications being used. Diagnosis is often more difficult in the elderly; denial of problems is frequent. Age-related changes in the pharmacokinetics of drugs with enhanced sensitivity to drugs and use of multiple drugs contribute to more severe consequences of substance abuse in the elderly. Substance abuse in the elderly may have late onset in reaction to the stresses of advanced age, including retirement, losses of spouse and friends, and problems with health. Chronic heavy alcohol and substance abuse often leads to premature death, which may in part account for reduction of incidence of chronic alcoholism in the elderly. In addition to selective survival, it has also been postulated that cohort differences contribute to different patterns of cultural acceptances of substance use in different generations. This hypothesis would be consistent with future increases in geriatric alcoholism.

## SPECIAL PROBLEMS IN DIAGNOSIS

Alcoholism is less likely to be detected in retired people because impairments in social and occupational functioning may not be as obvious. There are frequently fewer antisocial problems, and it may be difficult to distinguish the consequences of substance use from aging itself. Cognitive problems are frequent in the elderly in general. Even though they are accelerated by alcoholism, they may be misattributed to degenerative brain disease. The hazards of heavy alcohol use on sleep, sexual functioning, and cognitive ability potentiate these changes that ordinarily occur with aging.

## COMPLICATIONS

Alcohol's liver effects potentiate the possibility of overdose and, with some drugs, may lead to more rapid metabolism and affect the clinical effectiveness of medications needed by the elderly. Alcohol's depressant effects may further contribute to major depression and cognitive impairment. For some elderly patients, there is a loss of tolerance, which leads to greater effects with relatively small doses.

## TREATMENT ISSUES

In terms of treatment, elderly patients often respond better than younger addicts and alcoholics. This may be especially true of late-onset alcoholism. The programs generally include the same modalities as for other groups. However, there needs to be greater creativity, flexibility, and sensitivity to the needs of the elderly. Geriatric patients may need to be protected from threatening and acting-out behaviors of younger patients. Patients also require somewhat less confrontation and a greater degree of support and greater attention to work with family members. The consequences of divorce are likely to also be greater in this group, and spouses are less likely to do well if left because of a drinking problem (8).

## PRESCRIPTION DRUG ABUSE

Abuse of prescription drugs is a common problem in the elderly. One-fourth of geriatric patients are on psychoactive medications. Polypharmacy and sensitivity to toxic effects frequently lead elderly patients to get into difficulty. It is not infrequent that stopping medications may lead an apparent dementia to resolve. Benzodiazepine abuse among women is common, and sleep medications contribute to the problem. Memory problems may lead to unintentional misuse and overuse of prescription drugs. Inadequate explanation of the way medication should be taken and misunderstanding of dosage instructions are other problems. Nursing home patients are sometimes overmedicated to reduce disruptiveness and to facilitate reduction of need for nursing staff.

## ■ CHRONIC, HANDICAPPED, AND HOMELESS PATIENTS

Chronic psychoactive substance-dependent patients include a group with polysubstance abuse and with a wide range of choice of substances, exposure to treatment, and demographic characteristics. A common feature is maladaptive use of drugs of abuse over a long period of time exceeding at least a year with recurrent disability in physical, social, academic, or vocational functioning. This population frequently is in need of long-term institutional treatment, and there is a paucity of resources available for sophisticated, targeted treatment to the multiple challenges the population frequently confronts. Specific treatments and combinations of treatments have not established clear effectiveness, and the problems posed by this population are serious.

The chronic patient has been severely stigmatized, in part, possibly because the condition is seen as self-inflicted. However, unlike other maladaptive behavior—such as cigarette smoking (leading to emphysema) or lack of compliance with a low-salt diet (contributing to congestive heart failure)—the self-inflicted aspect of addiction has led to prejudice with regard to allocation of resources and handling of benefits and disability. This population may need a wide range of services and links with other programs in the community. Programs need to be culturally relevant and meet local realities of communities. Highly trained staff with positive attitudes about treatment are needed for implementing treatment of patients with multiple problems.

## COGNITIVELY IMPAIRED CHRONIC PATIENTS

The cognitive impairment that is associated with chronic alcohol and drug dependence is likely to affect the ability of patients to handle cognitive treatment programs. In addition, patients with Korsakoff's syndrome, alcohol dementia, and other severe complications of alcoholism and drug abuse may be in need of chronic nursing home care. Many treatment failures in alcohol- and drug-treatment programs are based on unappreciated difficulties that patients have in processing information.

## CHRONIC MENTAL PATIENTS WITH SUBSTANCE ABUSE

Chronic mental illness frequently contributes to the chronicity and severity of substance abuse problems. Facilities that combine psychiatric treatment with substance abuse rehabilitation techniques are often not available to these patients. Severely disturbed drug abusers may be shunned by drug rehabilitation facilities not equipped to handle them. Confrontational methods and emphasis on a drug-free model, which in some facilities includes underprescribing of psychotropic medication, can be detrimental to the mentally ill.

## CHRONIC SUBSTANCE ABUSE IN THE MULTI-DISABLED AND PHYSICALLY HANDICAPPED

Alcohol and drug abuse may contribute to the development of another physical handicap, such as paraplegia or head trauma. The physically disabled patient may have easier access to prescription drugs, and physicians may too readily prescribe medication out of a sense of guilt or futility. Disabled individuals who feel frustrated and angry at being dependent, socially isolated, and discriminated against by the rest of society may be more vulnerable to depression, anxiety, self-hatred, low motivation, and low self-esteem. They are more likely to suffer from chronic pain, and this may lead to iatrogenic addiction.

## BLIND AND DEAF PATIENTS

Blind and visually impaired patients may have problems coping with their impairment, and this may contribute to substance abuse. Deaf patients may have greater denial of the existence of substance abuse problems within their community, are afraid of stigmatization in having an additional problem, and have a lack of adequate signs in sign language to symbolize drunkenness or sobriety. Innovative treatment programs using simultaneous translators in groups to mainstream deaf patients through alcohol rehabilitation programs have been tried. Unfortunately, there are few alcohol and drug counselors who are well trained in signing.

## PARAPLEGIC PATIENTS

The problems of alcohol and drug abuse in patients with spinal cord disabilities are significant. The spinal cord problems may have been caused by alcohol and substance abuse in the first place; physical problems such as decubitus ulcers are caused by immobility and poor nutrition, which may be worsened by substance abuse. The Veterans Administration at Long Beach, California, has a program geared to treat spinal cord, alcoholic patients which combines physical rehabilitation, group psychotherapy, and Twelve-Step recovery groups such as AA and Narcotics Anonymous (NA).

## THE MENTALLY RETARDED
## SUBSTANCE ABUSER

Mildly retarded patients (IQ 60 to 85) are concrete and easily manipulated and may have problems learning from experience. Most of these patients live in the community and may attempt to socialize in neighborhood bars viewed as warm and nonjudgmental. There may be a wish to feel accepted as part of a group. Alcohol and substance abuse are seen as a means of improving socialization. Treatment and prevention efforts need to take into account the special needs of this population. Poor verbal skills may make it more difficult for them to benefit from AA and NA meetings and group programs that involve cognitive approaches and education about drug abuse. There is a need for emphasis on provision of a high degree of acceptance, warmth, and emotional support in working with these patients. If the patients are able to learn that they cannot drink safely and if simple messages of not drinking are reinforced, then they may do very well in treatment.

## HOMELESS PATIENTS WITH ADDICTIONS

Evidence shows that the homeless population is no longer principally composed of skid row alcoholics or single, older, chronic alcoholic men (9). The population is getting younger and includes an increasing number of women; as many as 90 percent have a primary psychiatric diagnosis. In several different urban samples in the United States, 20 to 60 percent of homeless patients recorded alcohol dependence. These patients frequently do not receive welfare, are disconnected from a social network including families, and are unable to utilize available social services. They are often entering treatment through intervention by church groups, Twelve-Step programs, and after-hospital detoxification. Clinics that work with homeless substance abusers struggle with trying to get basic social support services with adequate provision for meals and a place to live.

## ■ MINORITIES

Alcohol and drug abuse is a major problem in subsets of minority populations (10). Psychoactive substance abuse has had a major impact on overall life expectancies in blacks, Hispanics, and native American Indians. Although compared to whites blacks have comparable rates of heavy drinking, blacks have suffered a disproportionate amount of medical, psychological, and social sequelae. Blacks have twice the rate of cirrhosis and 10 times the rate of esophageal cancer in the 35- to 44-year-old age group. Half of black homicide cases are alcohol related. The rates of substance abuse may be skewed somewhat due to statistics that rely heavily on public facilities. Blacks and Hispanics make up 12 and 7 percent of the US population but 26 and 14 percent of the AIDS victims, respectively. Excessive alcohol consumption is also reported among rural and urban native American Indians.

## TARGETING TREATMENT

Several researchers have been working in the area of minority substance abuse; however, there has been a paucity of information and data vitally needed in this area. We cannot assume that research and program design applicable to middle-class white Americans will be equally applicable to minority communities. There is a recognition of the need for culturally sensitive treatment programs in minority communities. What culturally sensitive means is open to research and discussion. There are some culturally specific etiologic and treatment-related problems. Unemployment, racism, poor self-esteem, corruption of cultural values, and economic exploitation are prevailing problems in urban black communities and may contribute to the high rates of psychoactive substance abuse. Blacks are more readily diagnosed as alcoholics than whites and are often misdiagnosed psychiatrically. Black teenagers report less alcohol abuse than white teenagers; however, they quickly catch up and have comparable rates of abuse in their 20s and 30s. Although the biopsychosocial approach is equally valid in minorities, social factors such as poor education, unemployment, low job skills, racism, and substance-abusing peer role models become important etiologic factors and need to be addressed in any culturally sensitive program. Recognition and cooperation of indigenous cultural institutions such as the black church are needed. Blacks have had less access to treatment in the past; cutbacks in funding of social agencies may further block access to treatment.

## CULTURAL PATTERNS

Native American Indians have a history of the concept of the "drinking party," in which alcohol is consumed to excess and disinhibition is sanctioned in that setting. Hispanics have the notion of machismo, where manhood is equated with the ability to hold one's liquor. If a man is able to provide for his family, alcoholism may be well tolerated. Alcohol is often seen as a celebration of life and integrally related to holidays and festivals. Exposure of alcoholism often brings shame to the family and the community.

Treatment in minority communities generally must focus more on the extended family. Treatment programs and AA meetings must have some flexibility and respond to cultural norms. We must also recognize the heterogenicity within the minority communities. For example, a rural southern American black may have different cultural norms compared to West Indian blacks. In addition, minority women may have different roles and special treatment issues that are not prevalent in the majority population.

In summary, treatment personnel are faced with combining good basic alcohol and drug abuse treatment with cultural sensitivity. In reality, alcohol and drugs are going to remain a major problem within minority communities until we adequately address basic social ills.

## ■ REFERENCES

1. Blume SB: Women and alcohol. JAMA 1986; 256:1467–1470
2. What science knows about AIDS: a single-topic issue. Scientific American 1988; October
3. Niven RG: Adolescent drug abuse. Hosp Community Psychiatry 1986; 37:596–607
4. Use of Licit and Illicit Drugs by American High School Students, 1975–1984. Rockville, MD, National Institute on Drug Abuse, 1985
5. Johnston LD, O'Malley PM, Bachman JG: National Trends in Drug Use and Related Factors Among American High School Students and Young Adults 1975–1986. Rockville, MD, National Institute on Drug Abuse, 1987
6. Amini F, Zellwing M, et al: A controlled study of inpatient versus outpatient treatment of delinquent drug abusing adolescents: one year results. Compr Psychiatry 1982; 23:436–443
7. American Psychiatric Association: Diagnostic and Statistical Manual of Mental Disorders, 3rd ed, revised. Washington, DC, American Psychiatric Association, 1987
8. Abrams RC, Alexopoulos GS: Alcohol and drug abuse: substance in the elderly over the counter and illegal drugs. Hosp Community Psychiatry 1988; 39:822–823
9. Koegel P, Burnam A: Alcoholism among homeless adults in the inner city of Los Angeles. Arch Gen Psychiatry 1988; 45:1011–1018
10. Minorities. Alcohol Health and Research World. 1986–1987; Winter

# INDEX